W9-BRR-611

Meredith® Press
An imprint of Meredith® Books

Simply Handmade™: 365 Easy Projects for Every Occasion

Editor: Carol Field Dahlstrom
Technical Editor: Susan M. Banker
Graphic Designer: Marisa Dirks
Copy Chief: Catherine Hamrick
Copy and Production Editor: Terri Fredrickson
Book Production Managers: Pam Kvitne, Marjorie J. Schenkelberg
Contributing Copy Editor: Diane Doro
Contributing Proofreaders: Sheila Mauck, Debra Morris Smith, Margaret Smith
Photographers: Andy Lyons Cameraworks, Pete Krumhardt, Scott Little
Technical Illustrator: Chris Neubauer Graphics, Inc.
Electronic Production Coordinator: Paula Forest
Editorial and Design Assistants: Judy Bailey, Mary Lee Gavin,
Karen Schirm

Meredith® Books
Editor in Chief: James D. Blume
Design Director: Matt Strelecki
Managing Editor: Gregory H. Kayko

Director, Retail Sales and Marketing: Terry Unsworth
Director, Sales, Special Markets: Rita McMullen
Director, Sales, Premiums: Michael A. Peterson
Director, Sales, Retail: Tom Wierzbicki
Director, Sales, Home & Garden Centers: Ray Wolf
Director, Book Marketing: Brad Elmitt
Director, Operations: George A. Susral
Director, Production: Douglas M. Johnston

Vice President, General Manager: Jamie L. Martin

***Better Homes and Gardens®* Magazine**
Editor in Chief: Jean LemMon
Executive Food Editor: Nancy Byal

Meredith Publishing Group
President, Publishing Group: Christopher M. Little
Vice President, Finance & Administration: Max Runciman

Meredith Corporation
Chairman and Chief Executive Officer: William T. Kerr

Chairman of the Executive Committee: E. T. Meredith III

All of us at Better Homes and Gardens® Books are dedicated to providing you with information and ideas to create beautiful and useful projects. We welcome your comments and suggestions. Write to us at: Better Homes and Gardens Books, Crafts Editorial Department, 1716 Locust St., Des Moines, IA 50309-3023.

Cover photography: Andy Lyons
Cover projects: Charming Note Cards, page 198; Rainbow Cup and Trivet, page 148;
Back cover projects: Frosted Pumpkin, page 10; Gilded Ornaments, pages 84–85; Oh-So-Cute Baby Shoes, page 181
Inside front cover projects: Color Burst Seed Balls, page 128; Elegant Wedding Candle, page 126; Leaf-Laden Pots, page 56
Inside back cover projects: Bow-Topped Valentine, page 113; Season's Greetings Coasters, page 74; Silver-Trimmed Pots, page 189

First Edition.
Printing Number and Year: 10 9 8 7 6 5 4 3 2 1   10 09 08 07 06 05 04 03 02 01 00
Library of Congress Catalog Card Number: 00-132133
ISBN: 0-696-21037-1

simply handmade

Throughout the seasons we are blessed with reasons to celebrate—special occasions and holidays, when we remember those close at heart. Some of these reasons to celebrate are holidays marked on the calendar that we look forward to every year—Halloween, Thanksgiving, Christmas, and Easter. But some are events that are more personal, such as a graduation, a special thank you, or welcoming a new baby.

We love to celebrate the seasons and share our talents by creating gifts and decorations that bring happiness to ourselves and to others for every occasion. *Simply Handmade* offers exciting new ideas for you to make for every happy event.

Some of the ideas are projects that teach you a new technique—some are ideas you can make in minutes with supplies from around the house—and some are so quick, you can create them while waiting for guests to arrive. So come along and find a reason to celebrate—every day of the year.

Carol Field Dahlstrom

pages 8–59

As summer breezes fade and the glories of autumn come alive, enjoy a variety of quick-and-easy fall projects to make and love. You'll discover bright new ways to celebrate autumn holidays and share your talents with those you hold dear.

fall

winter

pages 60–123

The season of giving offers joyous opportunities to create gifts and decorations from the heart. From etched Christmas coasters for wintertime entertaining to ornaments to make by the dozens, you'll find hours of fun in this inspiring chapter.

pages 124–173

Spring is the perfect time to begin fresh, new projects—for indoors and out! Come along as we celebrate the warmth of the season with projects for Easter, gift giving, and decorating your spring home.

spring

summer

pages 174–211

Inspired by the long-awaited beauty of summer, this chapter will tempt your passion for tiling, sewing, painting, and more. You may discover a new technique to try or an old favorite that will let your talent shine.

about this book...

In this inspiring book you'll find fun projects to make for every season and occasion throughout the year. You can share your talents by creating lovely gifts that look like they took a lot of time (only you need to know how really simple they were to make!). Most of the projects can be completed in an evening or less with readily available supplies. To help you plan your creative time, we've divided the projects into three categories:

For last-minute showstoppers...

...look for a *Good Ideas* project. These quick-as-a-wink ideas often use supplies you have on hand.

Celebrate special occasions and holidays year-round by making

When you have a free evening...

make it in minutes

oh-so-cute baby shoes

Imagine how precious your little angel will look wearing these whimsically painted shoes.

To make the shoes you will need:
White baby shoes
Glossy acrylic paints in lime green, teal green, lavender, black, white, turquoise, yellow, and pink
Small flat paintbrushes
Fine liner brush

here's how **To make this project,** begin with a clean white pair of baby shoes. Remove shoelaces before painting.

To paint the striped decorative edge around bottom, paint a solid area first in lime green. Let the paint dry. Add stripes over top using teal green and a small flat paintbrush. Let the paint dry. Add lavender stripes over teal green using a narrower fine paintbrush. Let dry.

Paint the shoe top/tongue solid black. Let dry. Add white dots by dipping the handle end of paintbrush into paint and dotting on the surface.

Paint the side panels turquoise. Let dry. Paint a yellow sun on the turquoise. Paint a circle first, then make short strokes around circle with a fine paintbrush.

Paint pink and yellow stripes around top, and trim with pink and yellow checks around stitched areas. Let dry. Lace with colored laces.

1 more idea...
- Use a permanent marker to write nursery rhymes sayings around the shoes, using the seams as guides.

also try this...
- For your little sports fan, write, "Go, Team!" in the appropriate team colors on the shoes.

180

181

...choose a *Make It in Minutes* project. Your success is guaranteed with our easy-to-follow, step-by-step instructions.

Master a new and easy technique...

frosted pumpkin

step-by-step

Frost is on the pumpkin...and your awaited guests will know winter is near when this glistening pumpkin greets them at the door.

To make a pumpkin you will need:
Clean pumpkin
White dimensional fabric paint
White glitter

1 **Choose a pumpkin** with a shape you like and a long, interesting stem. Clean and dry the pumpkin.

2 **Using a bottle of white dimensional paint,** apply a generous amount of paint to the raised ridges of the stem and some of the lines extending down from the stem. Paint the lines on the pumpkin at varying lengths, about one-third of the way down the pumpkin. Add more white paint around the pumpkin stem, if desired. Work fairly quickly so you can complete all painting before any of it dries.

3 **Draw as many snowflakes as you wish.** To make a snowflake, first draw an X shape.

4 **Add a third line horizontally** across the center of the X to make a six-sided snowflake. Begin all snowflakes this way, then add dots and smaller lines, or whatever you wish to make the flakes look different. After painting snowflakes, add random white dots between the snowflakes.

5 **While the paint is wet,** sprinkle white glitter over the painted areas. Let the paint dry. Brush off excess glitter.

1 more idea...
- For a Halloween version of this pumpkin, use black paint and glitter and make spiders and webs instead of snow.

also try this...
- For a quick centerpiece, place a frosted pumpkin on a large white paper doily sprinkled with artificial snow.

10

11

...when you try a *Step-by-Step* project. Our helpful photographs will show you exactly what to do to create your own masterpiece.

wonderful gifts and decorations that share your creative talents!

In creating, the only hard thing is to begin;
A grass blade is no easier to make than an oak.

—— JAMES RUSSELL LOWELL

Celebrate the glorious bounty and joy-filled holidays that abound during this color-struck season. Whether you choose a carved pumpkin or a lovely autumn centerpiece, enjoy creating trims that bring the beauty of the outdoors in.

fall

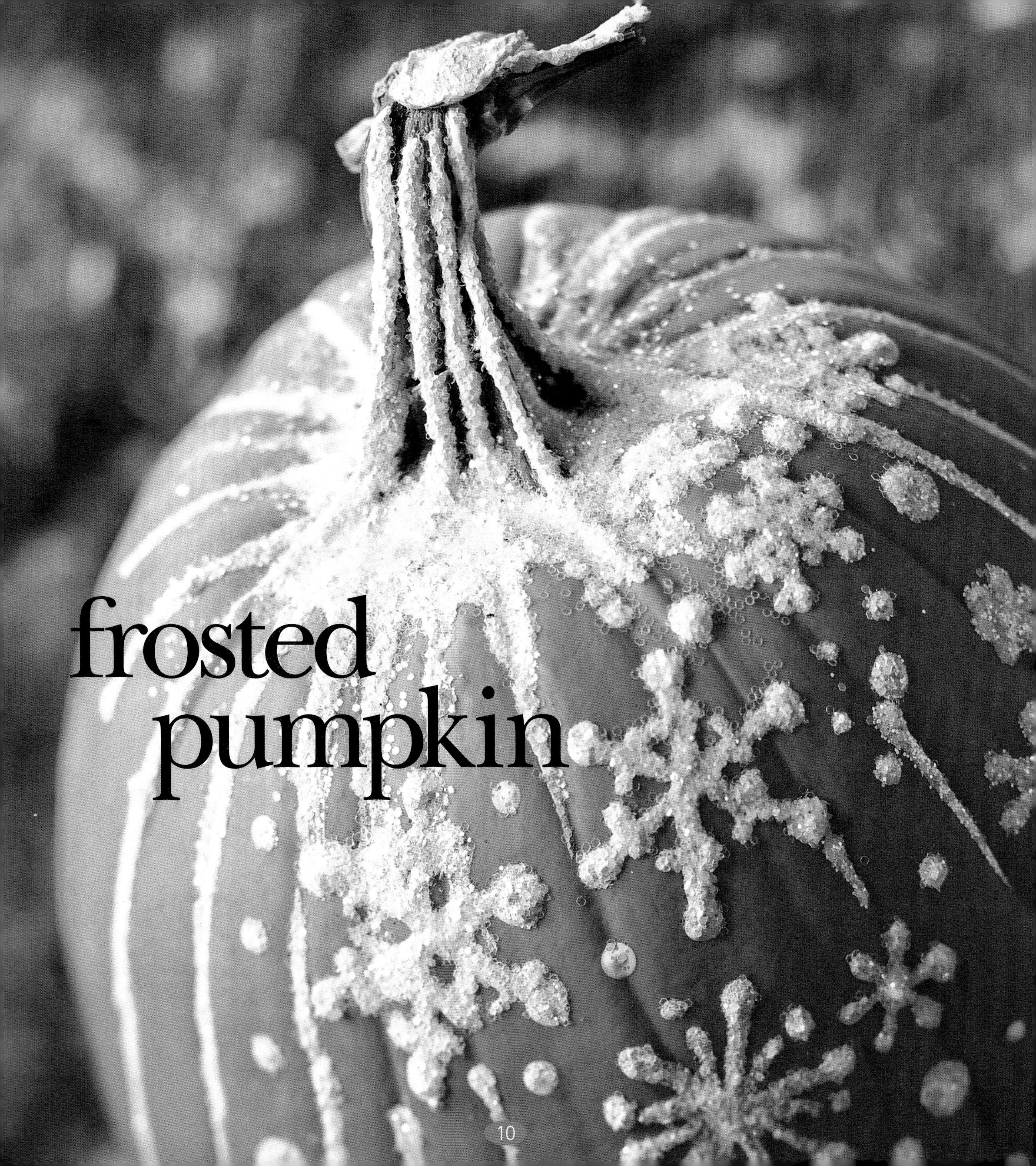

frosted pumpkin

Frost is on the pumpkin...and your awaited guests will know winter is near when this glistening pumpkin greets them at the door.

To make a pumpkin you will need:
Clean pumpkin
White dimensional fabric paint
White glitter

1 Choose a pumpkin with a shape you like and a long, interesting stem. Clean and dry the pumpkin.

2 Using a bottle of white dimensional paint, apply a generous amount of paint to the raised ridges of the stem and some of the lines extending down from the stem. Paint the lines on the pumpkin at varying lengths, about one-third of the way down the pumpkin. Add more white paint around the pumpkin stem, if desired. Work fairly quickly so you can complete all painting before any of it dries.

3 Draw as many snowflakes as you wish. To make a snowflake, first draw an X shape.

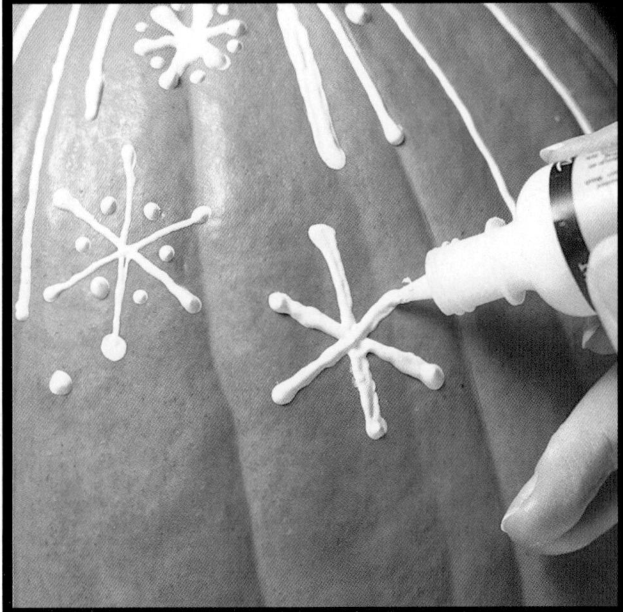

4 Add a third line horizontally across the center of the X to make a six-sided snowflake. Begin all snowflakes this way, then add dots and smaller lines, or whatever you wish to make the flakes look different. After painting snowflakes, add random white dots between the snowflakes.

5 While the paint is wet, sprinkle white glitter over the painted areas. Let the paint dry. Brush off excess glitter.

1 more idea...

- For a Halloween version of this pumpkin, use black paint and glitter and make spiders and webs instead of snow.

also try this...

- For a quick centerpiece, place a frosted pumpkin on a large white paper doily sprinkled with artificial snow.

ring-around-the-candleholder

A clever concoction for a Halloween tabletop, these napkin-ring candleholders are painted with fingernail polish.

To make the candleholders you will need:
- Round wood napkin rings in desired height
- 3-inch wood disks, if desired
- Newspapers
- Nail polish in black, white, purple, orange, and green (glitter polish, if desired)
- Hot-glue gun and hot-glue sticks
- Votive, floating, or taper candles

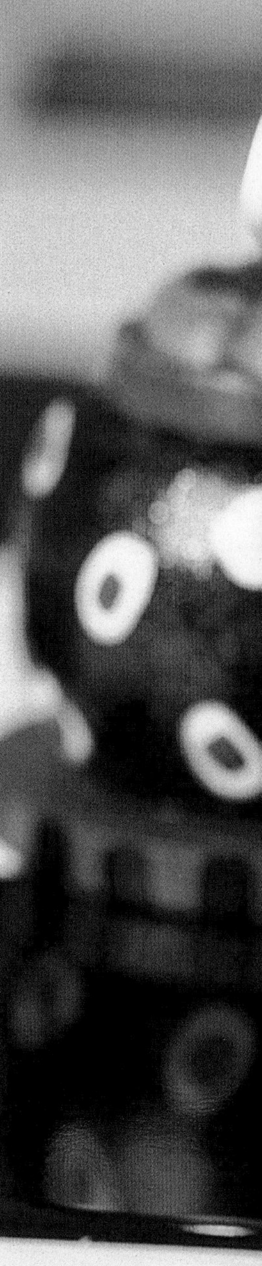

1 more idea...
- Use acrylic paints to decorate the napkin rings. Lightly sand the napkin-ring surface before painting to be sure the acrylic paint adheres.

also try this...
- For fun individual treat cups, make short versions of this project, gluing a paper circle to the bottom.

here's how **To make this project,** decide how to stack the napkin rings to make a candleholder. Use wood disks as the base, if desired. DO NOT glue together yet.

Cover the work surface with newspapers. Paint each of the rings separately, using the photograph for ideas. Start with a base coat and let it dry. Then add the dots, stripes, or whatever motifs you desire. Let the nail polish dry. Paint the wood disks in the same manner.

Use hot glue to secure the napkin rings together. Let the glue dry. Place a candle in or on top of the holder. Do not let the flame get close to the holder.

beaded pumpkin

Beads add an elegant touch and make this duo of Halloween pumpkins the pick of the crop.

To make a set of pumpkins you will need:

Large and small pumpkins
Beaded garland
Straight pins
Wide wire-edged ribbon
Star sequins
Quilting pins
Beading wire
Beads

here's how **To make the large beaded pumpkin,** attach one end of beaded garland at the top of the pumpkin at the base of the stem. Hold the garland in place with a pin. Loop the garland down approximately halfway and bring back up to the stem and pin in place. Continue making loops around the entire pumpkin top. Tie a generous bow made from wide wired ribbon around the stem.

To make the small beaded pumpkin, attach star sequins randomly using quilting pins to secure. Make three beaded strands by threading beads on lengths of wire. Add a star sequin to the ends, if desired. Secure one end of the wire to hold the beads in place. Leave 1 inch of wire at the opposite end to poke into the pumpkin next to the stem.

1 more idea...

- Use star garland instead of beaded garland for the large pumpkin.

also try this...

- For a quicker version of the small pumpkin, delete the beaded strands and use only the star sequins.

vibrant fall centerpiece

Use the bottom half of a pumpkin to create this glorious centerpiece for family and friends to gather around.

To make the centerpiece you will need:

Pumpkin
Sharp knife
Spoon
Pencil
Water
Flowers
Floral spray paint, optional
Vines
Artificial grapes

here's how **To make this project,** choose a nicely shaped pumpkin with a solid symmetrical base so it sits well. Cut the top one-third of the pumpkin off with a knife. Cut around the pumpkin so that it is about the same height all the way around. Clean out the inside with a spoon. Using a pencil, mark even intervals around the top outer edge of the pumpkin where you would like to cut pointed shapes into the pumpkin. When you have drawn these, cut the pointed peaks and discard the extra pieces.

Place a plastic liner in the pumpkin and fill with clear, cool water. Fill with any kind of flowers you wish. Reds, greens, and purples are attractive with an orange pumpkin. The red flowers shown here are stems from sedum plants. The reds in the flowers were enhanced with a light spray of a vibrant deep red floral spray paint. Combine a variety of colors and textures of fresh and dried flowers and weeds. Add graceful vines, draping some around the base of the pumpkin. Add artificial purple grapes at the base of the pumpkin.

1 more idea...

- For a last-minute centerpiece, use an ice pick to punch holes in the top of the pumpkin to insert the flower stems.

also try this...

- Fill a pumpkin with fresh fruit instead of flowers and vines.

good ideas *glitter-topped pumpkins*

Whether displayed outdoors or in, the sparkle of these pumpkins will set a festive mood. Paint the stems with glue and sprinkle on metallic glitter. Add a twist of silver curling ribbon and the pumpkins shine.

ready-*for*-school hairpins

Young ladies will look classy in class with these clay-trimmed pins prettying up their hair.

To make a hairpin you will need:
Bakeable colored clay, such as Sculpey, in purple, magenta, hot pink, teal blue, green, pink, and light blue
Small sharp knife
Small rhinestones
Fine iridescent white glitter
Large bobby pins, about 3 inches long
Shallow glass baking dish
Instant-bond glue, such as Super Glue

1 **Make leaves** from small pieces of green clay. Form into small ovals and flatten. Pinch one end of the leaf shape to form a point. Using a small sharp knife, lay flat against the center of leaf shape and press gently to make the center crease of leaf.

2 **Using very small portions of clay,** create tiny flowers. Make small pea shapes and flatten. Roll out a single long strand of clay to about the width of a round toothpick and coil into a flower shape.

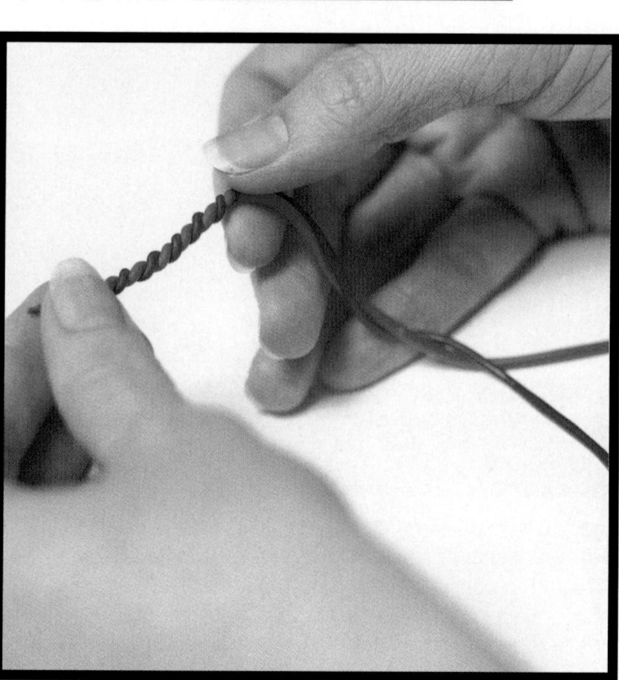

3 **To make the two-color** portion of the flower, roll out two strands of clay. Hold together at one end and twist until entwined. Wrap around a flattened flower shape. If desired, add contrasting clay centers or press in rhinestones.

4 **If desired, rub glitter** into the surface of the flowers.

5 **Arrange flowers and leaves** into a strip on bobby pin, gently pressing together. Place in a dish and bake according to the manufacturer's instructions. Allow to cool before handling.

6 **Gently remove clay pieces** from bobby pin. Apply a thin line of glue to the pin and attach the strip of flowers. Do not let glue seep inside the bobby pin. Let dry before wearing.

1 more idea...
- Customize hairpins to match school colors or coordinate with a favorite shirt.

also try this...
- Embellish barrettes and plastic headbands in the same manner.

make it in minutes

"bootiful" napkin rings

When the Halloween goodies are to be served, these playful napkin rings will be the talk of the table.

To make the napkin rings you will need:

- Chenille stems in desired colors
- Jack-o'-lantern jingle bells, plastic spiders, or other small Halloween trims
- Empty paper tube
- Thick white crafts glue

here's how **To make this project,** choose three different colors of chenille stems. Twist the chenille stems together at one end to secure.

Braid the chenille stems together. If using a jingle bell, slip it over one of the chenille stems when braided halfway around. Continue braiding to the end and twist the ends together. Wrap the braid around a paper tube to form a napkin ring. Glue on Halloween trims as desired. Let the glue dry.

1 more idea...

- For a kids' Halloween party, have the guests make bracelets in the same manner.

also try this...

- For coordinating napkins, cut squares from Halloween fabrics using pinking shears.

goody sacks

Surprise treat seekers with these clever paper bags filled with Halloween goodies.

here's how **To make this project,** trace the patterns, *pages 22–23*, onto tracing paper. Transfer the witch and cat pattern to black paper, the pumpkin to orange paper, and the pumpkin eyes, nose, and mouth to yellow paper. Cut out the shapes.

Tear the yellow, orange, and green background papers the same size as the pattern. Crimp the background papers with a paper crimper.

Glue the cat to the yellow background paper, the witch to the orange background paper, and the pumpkin to the green background paper. Glue the eyes, mouth, and nose on the pumpkin. Draw lines on the pumpkin with red marking pen.

Sew two yellow beads for the cat's eyes. Sew the buttons on the background papers and near the bottom edge of the paper bags as shown. Glue each design to a paper bag.

To make the goody sacks you will need:

Tracing paper
Pencil
Card stock or heavy paper in yellow, green, black, and orange
Scissors
Paper crimper
Glue stick
Red marking pen
2 yellow glass beads
Black thread
Sewing needle
Assorted buttons in green, yellow, orange, and black
5x8½-inch brown paper bags with handles

1 more idea...

- Personalize a goody bag by writing the recipient's name above the paper design.

also try this...

- For other Halloween motifs, trace around cookie cutters or images in coloring books.

goody sacks (continued)

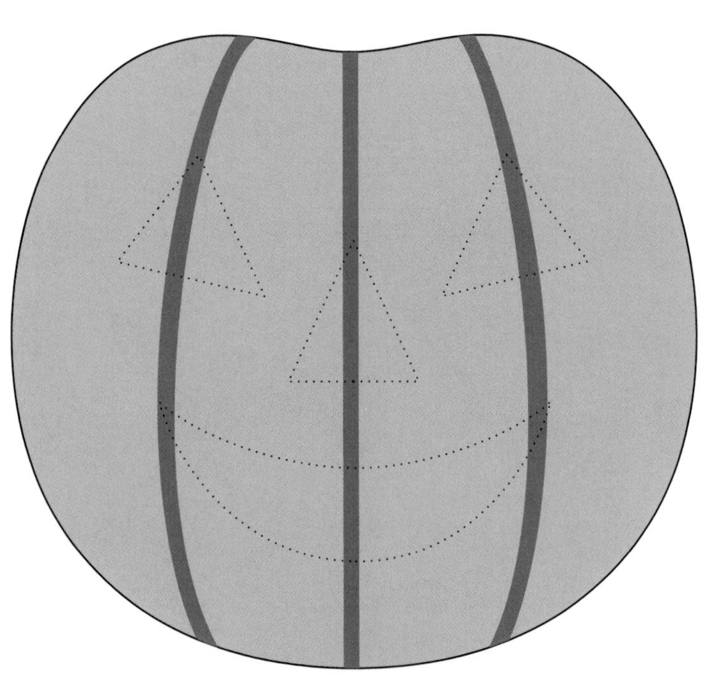

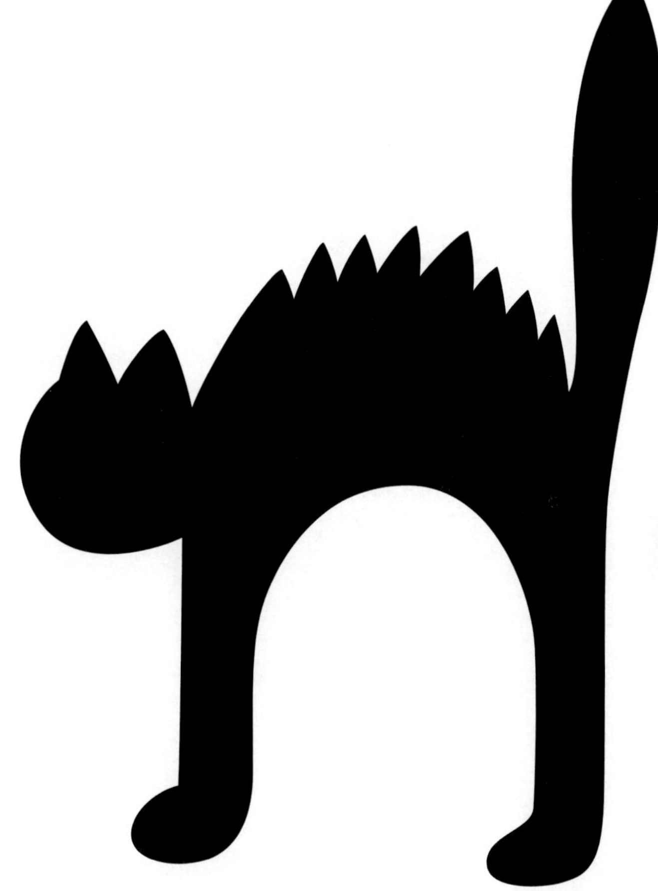

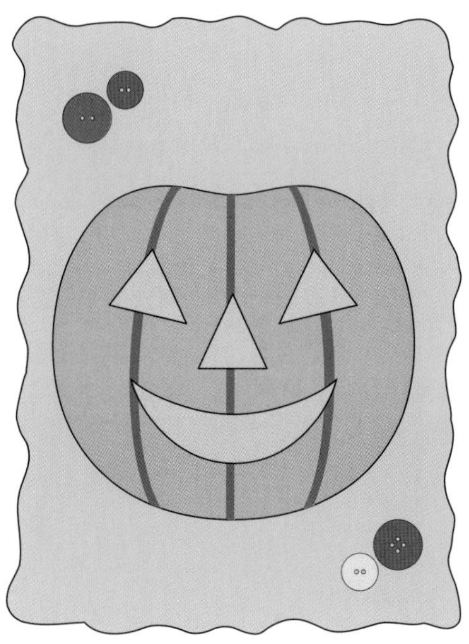

step-by-step

candy-filled cones

To make a treat holder you will need:
- Cone-shape paper drinking cups
- Pencil
- Thick white crafts glue
- Paintbrush
- Glitter in white, orange, gold, purple, and green
- Paper punch
- Metallic chenille stems in silver and gold

Paper drinking cups make creative Halloween treat holders when embellished with glitter and metallic chenille-stem handles.

1 **To make the candy-corn** version, divide the cup into thirds using a pencil. Paint the portion near the rim with glue.

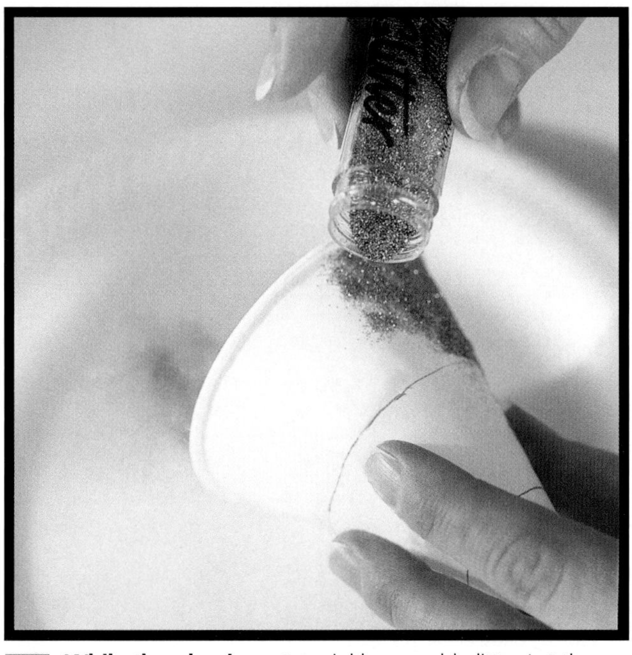

2 **While the glue is wet**, sprinkle on gold glitter. Let the glue dry. Paint the center portion of the cup with glue and sprinkle on orange glitter. Let dry. Paint glue on the tip and sprinkle with white glitter. Let dry.

3 **To make the swirl** version, paint the entire cup with glue. Sprinkle purple glitter over the entire surface. Let dry. Draw a swirl with glue on one side of the cup. Sprinkle with green glitter. Let dry.

4 **To make holes for a handle**, punch two holes in the paper cup, opposite each other and just below the rim. Thread a chenille stem through the two holes, forming a handle. Twist the ends to secure in place.

1 more idea...
- Use flat-bottomed paper cups and eliminate the handle for a quicker version of the holders.

also try this...
- Trim the cups with spider, skeleton, and ghost motifs.

spooky pumpkins

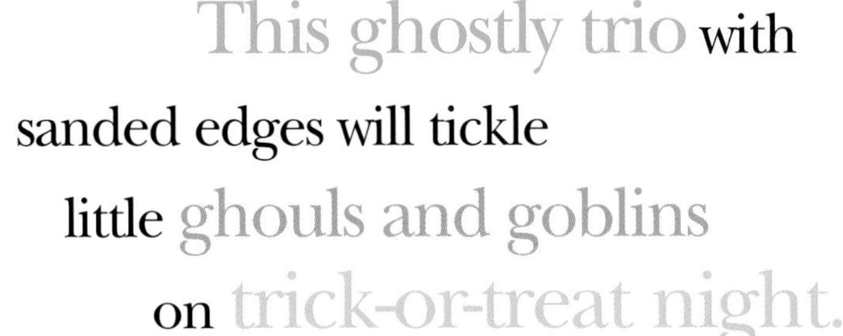

This ghostly trio with sanded edges will tickle little ghouls and goblins on trick-or-treat night.

here's how **To make this project,** enlarge and trace the patterns, *pages 28–29*. Use a copy machine and enlarge each pattern at 200 percent or create the patterns with tracing paper and the grid scale. Transfer the patterns to the 1-inch pine.

Cut out the pumpkin shapes using a band saw. Use a jigsaw to cut out the face details. Remove sawdust using a tack cloth.

Paint the pumpkins white. Let the paint dry. Sand the edges as desired to create a worn look.

To make the pumpkins you will need:

- Tracing paper
- Pencil
- 1-inch-thick pieces of pine
- Band saw
- Jigsaw
- Tack cloth
- White acrylic paint
- Paintbrush
- Medium sandpaper

1 more idea...

- Place a picture hanger on the back of each wood pumpkin to hang on the wall.

also try this...

- Set these cutouts along the trick-or-treat path, placing a small votive candle in a holder behind each pumpkin.

spooky pumpkins (continued)

1 Square = 1 inch

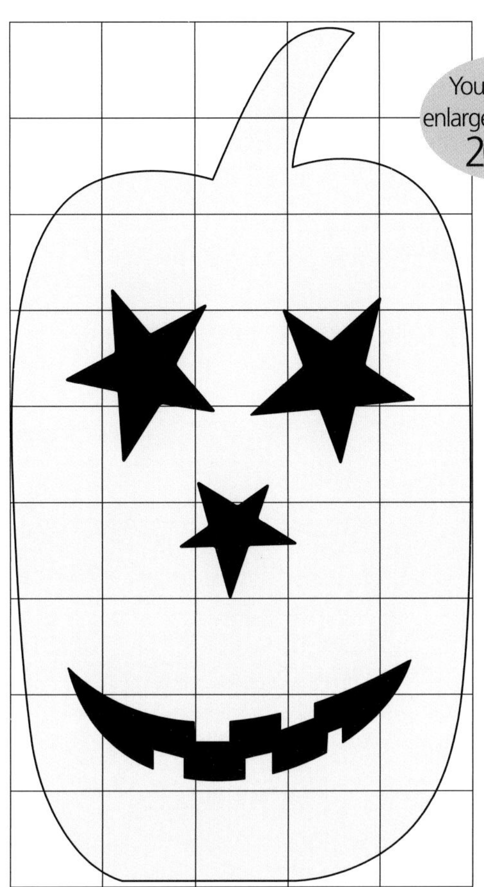

1 Square = 1 inch

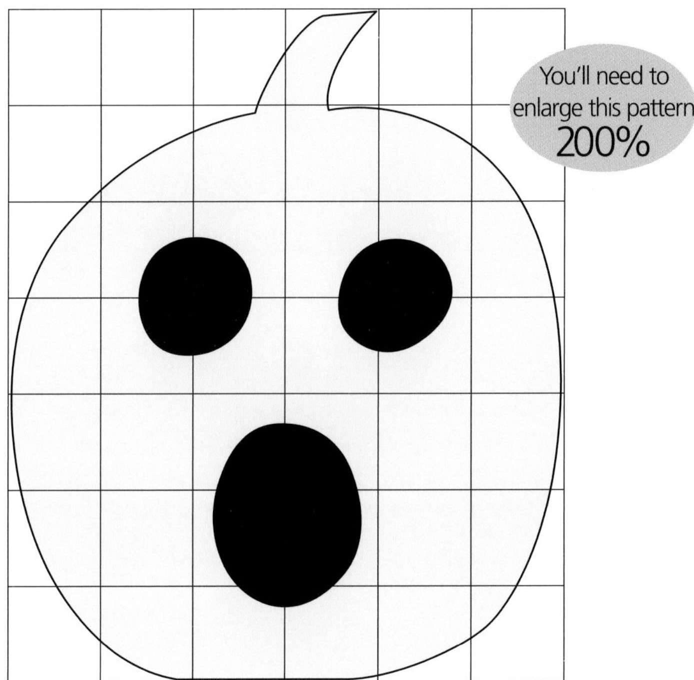

1 Square = 1 inch

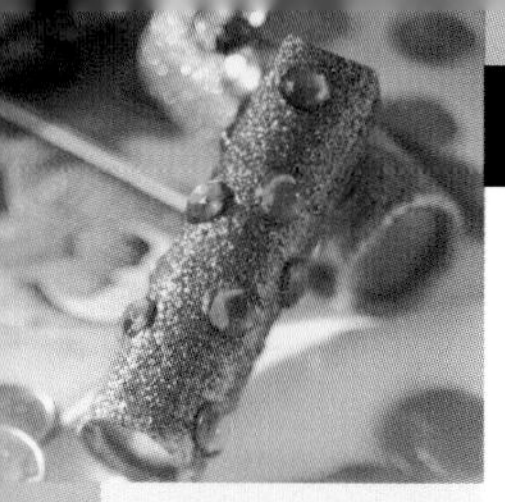

halloween surprise rolls

Trick-or-treaters of all ages will squeal with delight when these gem-studded money rolls hit their goody bags.

To make the money rolls you will need:
- Coins in a sleeve
- Thick white crafts glue
- Paintbrush
- Glitter
- Waxed paper
- Gems

1 more idea...
- Decorated in Christmas colors, these fun money rolls make unexpected stocking stuffers.

also try this...
- Get the kids involved and use Halloween stickers instead of glitter and gems to cover the money-roll sleeves.

here's how **To make this project,** begin with a full sleeve of coins. Use paintbrush to apply glue to the paper sleeve.

Sprinkle glitter over glue, covering the entire sleeve. Set the sleeve of coins on end on waxed paper and let the glue dry.

Glue gems as desired on one side of the glittered sleeve. Let the glue dry. Turn the sleeve over and add gems in the same manner. Let the glue dry.

peek-a-boo pumpkin

Fun for a Halloween party or any autumn get-together, these silly characters are right at home in their stout pumpkin birdhouse.

here's how **To make this project,** cut a small hole in the bottom of pumpkin. Remove the bottom piece of pumpkin shell. Clean out the inside of pumpkin using a spoon. Cut or drill five 1¼-inch holes, spaced randomly around the pumpkin.

To make the bird heads, paint each wooden ball with the desired color of acrylic paint and let dry. Glue on two small plastic eyes close together as shown, *left*.

To make the beaks, shape them from small pieces of clay. Use pieces about the size of a grape. Shape the clay into cones and clip once with scissors beginning at the tip. Do not clip all the way across. Spread the clay apart to form open beaks. Let the clay beaks dry. Paint the beaks yellow or black. Let the paint dry. Glue the beaks onto the bird heads below the eyes.

Cut five solder wire pieces 4 to 8 inches long. To form into a coil, wrap each around a large marking pen, 1-inch dowel, or similar object. Insert one end of the wire into the hole in the back of the wooden bird head, widening the hole with a pencil if needed. Glue the wire in place. Insert the other end of wire into the pumpkin inside each hole.

To make the pumpkin you will need:

Pumpkin
Spoon
Knife or drill with 1¼-inch drill bit
Acrylic paints in black, lavender, blue, green, pink, yellow, or other desired colors
Paintbrush
Five 1¼-inch wooden balls with flat end and tiny hole (doll heads)
Thick white crafts glue
¼-inch plastic moveable eyes
Crayola Model Magic clay
Scissors
Thick lead-free solder wire or armature wire
Wire cutters
Large marking pen, 1-inch dowel, or similar size tube shape

1 more idea...

- To display the pumpkin birdhouse, place it on a small pile of feathers.

also try this...

- For a more elegant version of this pumpkin, perch artificial feathered birds on the wires.

good ideas *jolly jack-o'-lanterns*

Carve a trio of pumpkin pals for a lighthearted Halloween display. To nestle the jack-o'-lanterns close together, trim off one side of each of the outer pumpkins so they can snuggle close to their pal in the center.

hydrangea pumpkin

A cloud of hydrangea makes a beautiful presentation for the Thanksgiving table when tucked into the top of a natural green and orange pumpkin.

To make the arrangement you will need:
Medium or large pumpkin
Sharp knife
Spoon
Fresh-cut or artificial hydrangea
Scissors

here's how **To make this project,** cut a circle around the pumpkin stem. Scoop out the pumpkin using a spoon.

Use scissors to cut the hydrangea stems to an appropriate length when placed inside the pumpkin. If using fresh-cut flowers, place a plastic liner in the pumpkin before arranging the flowers.

1 more idea...

- Use miniature pumpkins and one sprig of hydrangea to make trims for individual place settings.

also try this...

- Fill the pumpkin with cattails, a mound of large pinecones, or interesting twigs.

beads-'n'-wire trimmed pumpkin

In celebration of the first Thanksgiving, add an intricate Native American design to a stark white pumpkin.

To make the pumpkin you will need:
White pumpkin
26-gauge gold wire
Iridescent bugle beads in blue and white
Iridescent seed beads in blue and orange
Wooden skewer or ice pick

here's how **To make this project,** start with the beaded band. Cut several 1-inch-long pieces of wire to attach the bugle beads. Slip a blue bead onto a wire, center it, and bend the ends down. Press the ends into the pumpkin, about one-third of the way from the top. Continue adding bugle beads in a zigzag line around pumpkin until completed.

Add the white bugle beads in the same manner, adding alternating colors of seed beads to the ends. Insert these pieces vertically where each blue zigzag points down as shown.

To make coils from the stem to the beaded banding, cut 8-inch lengths (longer or shorter depending on the size of the pumpkin) of wire. Leaving 1 inch at each end, wrap the wire piece around a wooden skewer or ice pick. Remove and poke one end into the pumpkin next to the stem. Following a groove in the pumpkin, pull the wire down and poke the remaining end in the pumpkin, just above the beaded banding. Continue adding coils to the pumpkin top, following the grooves or as desired. Add 2-inch coils below the beaded banding as shown.

1 more idea...

- Trim an orange pumpkin with purple, black, and lime green beads.

also try this...

- For a more contemporary look, use colorful plastic-coated wires to make the long and short spirals.

colorful cattails

Turn the page for a stunning display idea.

Grace the Thanksgiving table with an unexpected bouquet of lovely painted cattails.

To make a cattail bouquet you will need:
Cattails
Scissors
Gesso (available in art and crafts stores where the painting supplies are located)
Metallic model car spray paint or bottled acrylic paints
Thick white crafts glue
Gold ribbon

1 **Pick cattails when dry and firm**, and before they begin to puff. Cut stems to desired length. Remove any loose shedding layers from the stems.

2 **Coat the brown tail portions** generously with a coat of gesso. Allow it to soak into the cattails. Let it dry.

3 **Paint the entire cattail** using bottled acrylic paint or spray paint. Let the paint dry.

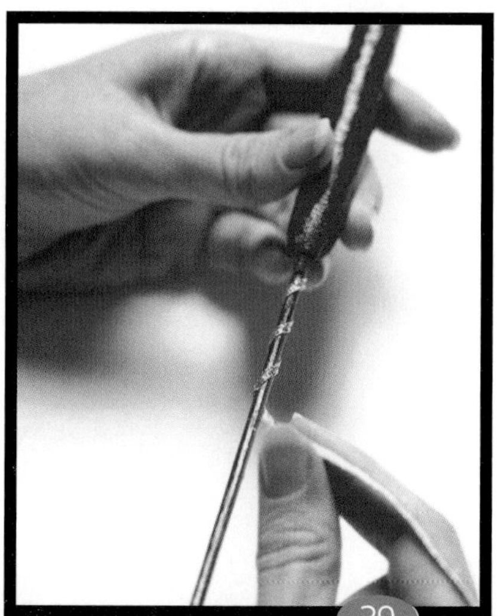

4 **Take a piece of narrow gold ribbon** and tie firmly to the top of stem. Wind the ribbon downward to the end of stem, holding in place with dabs of glue.

1 more idea...

- For a hearth decoration, cut the cattail stems short and arrange upright in a basket.

also try this...

- To quickly dress up unpainted cattails, wrap the stems with colored raffia and tie a bow at the top of each stem.

printed bottles

Towering bottles, printed with images of the season, make a welcome autumn housewarming gift.

To make a bottle you will need:

Bottles in colors such as red, gold, green, and orange
Acrylic paints in colors such as red, gold, green, and orange
Disposable foam plate
Leaf rubber stamp in desired design
Paper towel

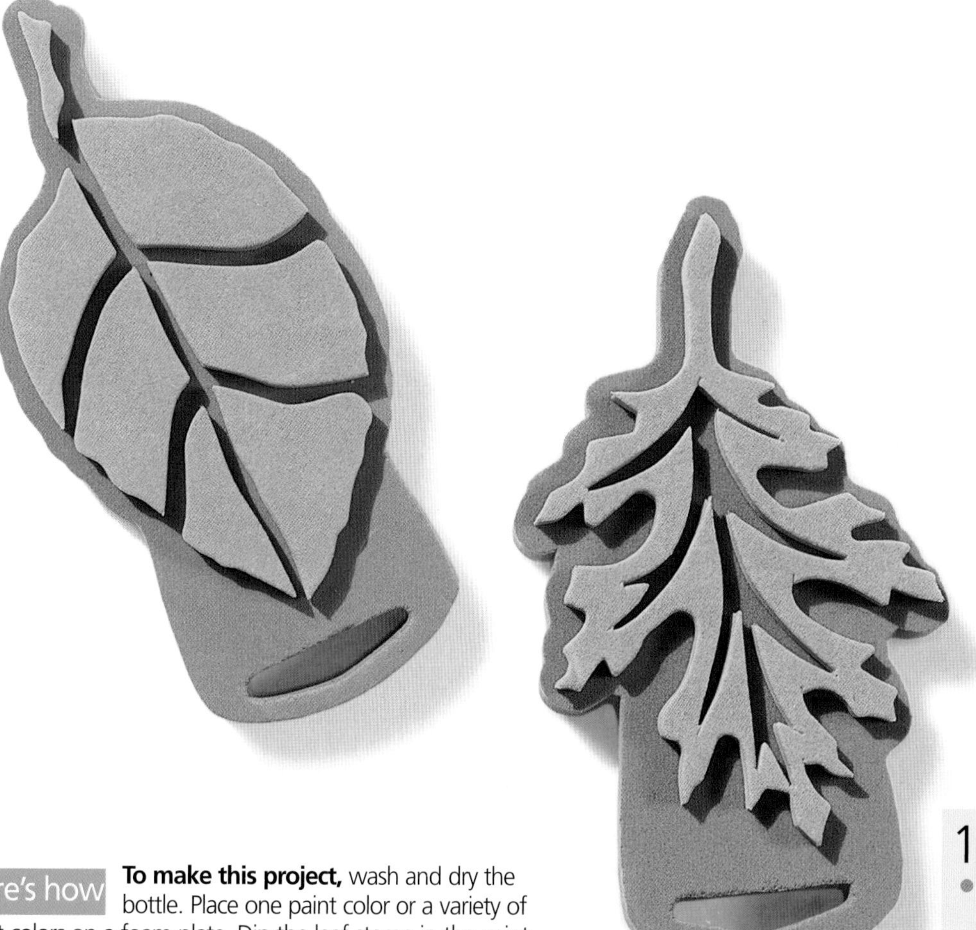

here's how **To make this project,** wash and dry the bottle. Place one paint color or a variety of paint colors on a foam plate. Dip the leaf stamp in the paint. Dab off once on a paper towel.

Press the stamp to the bottle and remove. Continue adding leaf images in this manner until the desired look is achieved. Let the paint dry.

1 more idea...

- To create a colored background on clear bottles, use model car spray paints.

also try this...

- Use these bottles as personalized gift containers for homemade salad dressings and liqueurs.

primitive luminarias

Greet your guests throughout the fall party season with these charming and primitive luminarias.

1 Gather items to be rusted. Apply a coat of metal surfacer to the cake pan inside and out using a disposable sponge brush. Apply a second coat when dry. Make sure all surfaces are covered. Let dry. Dispose of sponge applicator. Allow the iron finish to dry or cure for 12 hours or according to the product instructions.

2 Apply a coat of rust antiquing solution with sponge brush applicator. Allow to rust. Repeat another coat if more rust is desired. The more product added, the rustier the appearance. When rusting items, keep in mind that the orange or bright orange rust color will be toned down when the final coat of sealer is applied. You may want to test a small area first before applying the sealer. The sealer absorbs into the rust and darkens it to a brown color. An item cannot continue to rust after the sealer is applied.

3 Apply a coat of sealant. Brush over the entire area. Let dry and apply a second coat, if needed.

4 Prepare the metal can with the same steps used for the cake pan. When finished, punch nail holes into the side of the can in any pattern you desire.

5 Trace the star pattern, *below,* onto tracing paper, cut out, and trace onto tin four times. Cut out with scissors. Lay stars on a piece of thick cardboard and pound a sharp nail on one corner just enough to pierce a hole. Rust star shapes as in the previous steps, except you should not have to do the first step of applying the iron coat. Tin will rust easily using the rusting products.

6 Cut four pieces of wire, each 8 inches long. Coil each wire by winding around a pencil, then remove pencil.

7 Use an ice pick to poke four holes in opposite ends in the bottom of cake pan close to outer edge. Insert each coiled wire into a hole. Bend wire in place inside cake pan to hold it in place and prevent the wire from falling through. Attach other end of wire to the star.

8 Embellish the stars, can, and pan with various colored and shaped flat marbles. Attach to the sides with clear adhesive.

9 Choose an interesting piece of driftwood or post, cut off the top level, apply a generous amount of Liquid Nails adhesive to the flat end of wood, and attach the rusted pan. Let dry.

To make a candleholder you will need:
- 9-inch metal cake pan
- Metal can
- 2 disposable small sponge brushes
- Metal surfacer, such as Modern Options Instant Iron
- Rust antiquing solution, such as Modern Options Instant Rust
- Waterproof sealer
- Ice pick
- Tracing paper
- Pencil
- Scissors
- Thick cardboard
- Sharp nail
- Tin sheets
- 36-inch piece of thin wire
- Clear, waterproof adhesive
- Flat marbles in various shapes and sizes
- Wooden post or piece of driftwood
- Saw
- Construction-strength glue, such as Liquid Nails adhesive

1 more idea...
- Use this rusting method to add interest to fireplace screens, iron beds, and lamp bases.

also try this...
- Make small rusted stars, pierce the centers, and use pins to hold them in place on a pillar candle.

pilgrim hat place cards

Let your Thanksgiving guests know how glad you are they've joined you with these delightful, personalized place cards.

To make the place cards you will need:

- 3-inch terra-cotta flowerpots
- Acrylic paints in black, white, red, and blue
- Paintbrush
- Crafting foam in black, yellow, green, and purple
- Scissors
- Thick white crafts glue
- Black fabric paint pen

here's how **To make this project,** paint the entire pot black and allow it to dry. Choose a color to paint the band around the top of the pot. Let it dry. Make white dots on the rest of the pot by dipping the handle end of a paintbrush in white paint and dotting onto the surface.

Trace a circle from black foam about ½ inch wider all around than the pot opening, using an appropriate size dish, cup, or lid. Cut out.

To make the buckle, measure the width of the band of the pot (the portion painted a different color). Cut a rectangle from foam that measures about ⅛ inch deeper than the band on the pot. Cut out a smaller rectangle from the center. Glue the buckle to the band. Let the glue dry.

Use a black paint pen to write a name on the colored band. Allow the paint pen to dry before using.

1 more idea...

- Make a large version of this pilgrim hat for a centerpiece.

also try this...

- Use cone-shape paper cups to make witch hats at Halloween.

SARAH
MOM

This free-form fall centerpiece comes alive with a gathering of candles dancing in the center.

To make the centerpiece you will need:

Knife
Large pumpkin
Spoon
Ice pick
Small gourds, miniature pumpkins, and real or artificial berries
Toothpicks
Sand
Candles in desired sizes

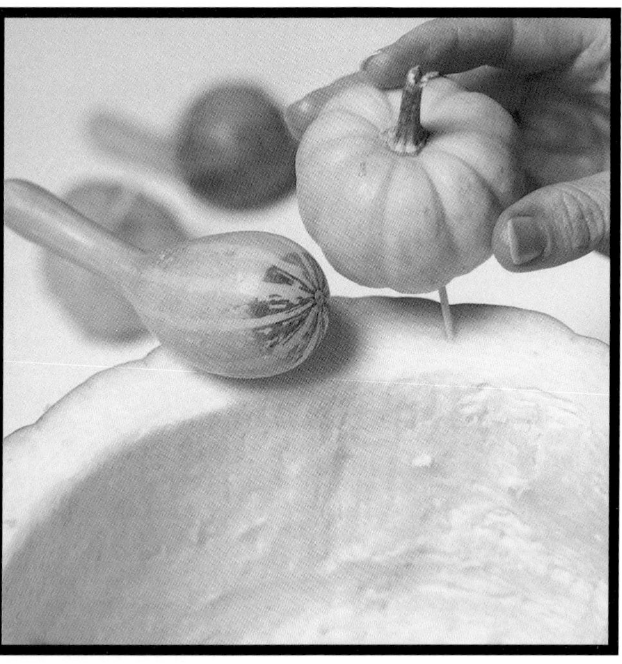

1 **Cut off the top of the pumpkin.** Clean out the inside with a spoon.

2 **Decide how the gourds,** miniature pumpkins, and berries will be arranged around the rim. Use an ice pick to poke a hole in the bottom of each gourd and small pumpkin. Place a toothpick into the hole and push into the rim of the large pumpkin where desired. Continue adding items in this manner until the rim is filled.

3 **Tuck berries between the gourds** and small pumpkins. Fill the bottom of the pumpkin with sand. Carefully arrange the candles in the sand.

1 more idea...

- Replace the candles with a bundle of interesting twigs or dried flowers.

also try this...

- For an everlasting version, use artificial berries and gourds glued on the rim of a foam pumpkin.

velveteen leaf pillows

The rich colors of the season are captured in beautiful accent pillows, made from soft fabrics and edged in gold.

To make one pillow you will need:

⅓ yard of cotton velveteen or velour
Dressmakers' pencil or fabric pen with disappearing ink
Scissors
⅓ yard of quilt batting
3 yards of gold cording
Thick white crafts glue
Fiberfill
Needle; thread
Bugle beads in gold, silver, and amber

here's how **To make this project** enlarge and trace the patterns, *pages 54–55*. Use a copy machine to enlarge each pattern at the percentage indicated, or create the patterns with tracing paper and the grid scale. Cut the fabric slightly larger than the leaf pattern. With fabric pen or pencil, trace around the leaf pattern on the right side of the fabric. Lay this fabric over a piece of quilt batting, right side up, and stitch the two layers together, following the drawn lines. Use the fabric pen or pencil to draw the veins of the leaf. DO NOT cut out the leaf. Baste a second piece of fabric to a piece of batting for the back of the pillow.

To make the veins, cut lengths of cording for the shorter veins first, cutting them ½ inch longer than the needed length. To prevent fraying, coat the ends of the cord with glue and let dry. Lay the veins over the drawn lines, butting one end of the cording to the line for the center vein, and allow the extra amount of cording to extend beyond the outside edge of the leaf. Using thread to blend with the cording, machine-zigzag the cord in place to the top of the leaf. Zigzag a piece of cording over the long, vertical vein making sure ½ inch of the cord extends beyond the top and bottom edge of the leaf.

Place the leaf front over the backing piece of fabric, right sides together. Pin securely and stitch the front and back together following the previous line of stitching on the leaf front. Leave an opening along one side for turning. Cut away excess fabric and batting; clip curves.

Turn leaf right side out and firmly stuff with fiberfill. Blindstitch the opening closed. Stitch bugle beads randomly to the front of the pillow.

Cut the remaining cording long enough to go around the entire edge of the leaf. Add glue to the ends of the cording and allow to dry. Apply glue to cording and glue around entire outside edge of the leaf. Use pins to hold cording in place while the glue dries.

1 more idea...

- For other seasons, make these pillows in the shapes of flowers, butterflies, or stars.

also try this...

- Make mini versions to stuff with potpourri instead of fiberfill for an autumn scented sachet.

velveteen leaf pillows (continued)

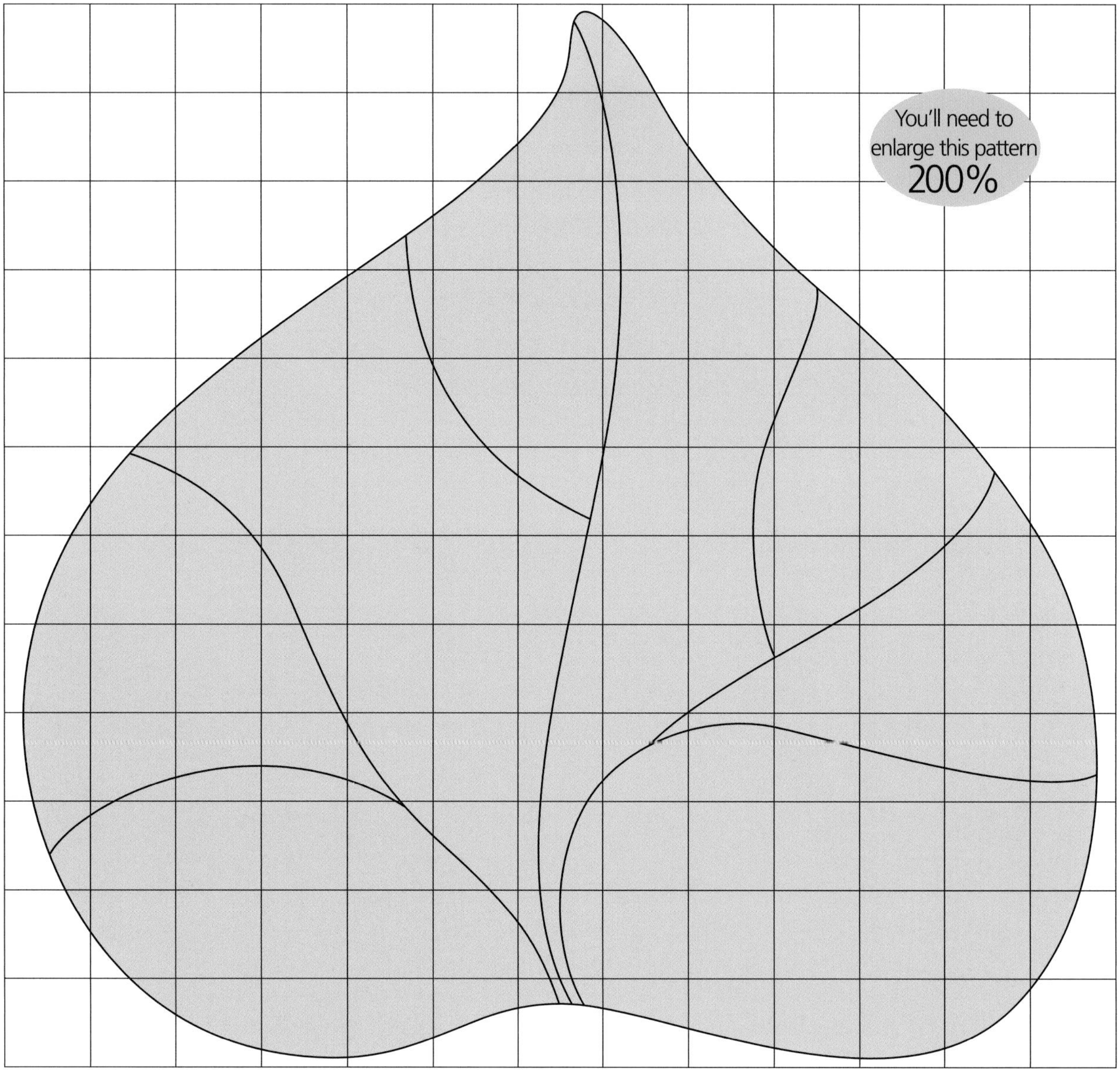

You'll need to enlarge this pattern 200%

1 Square = 1 inch

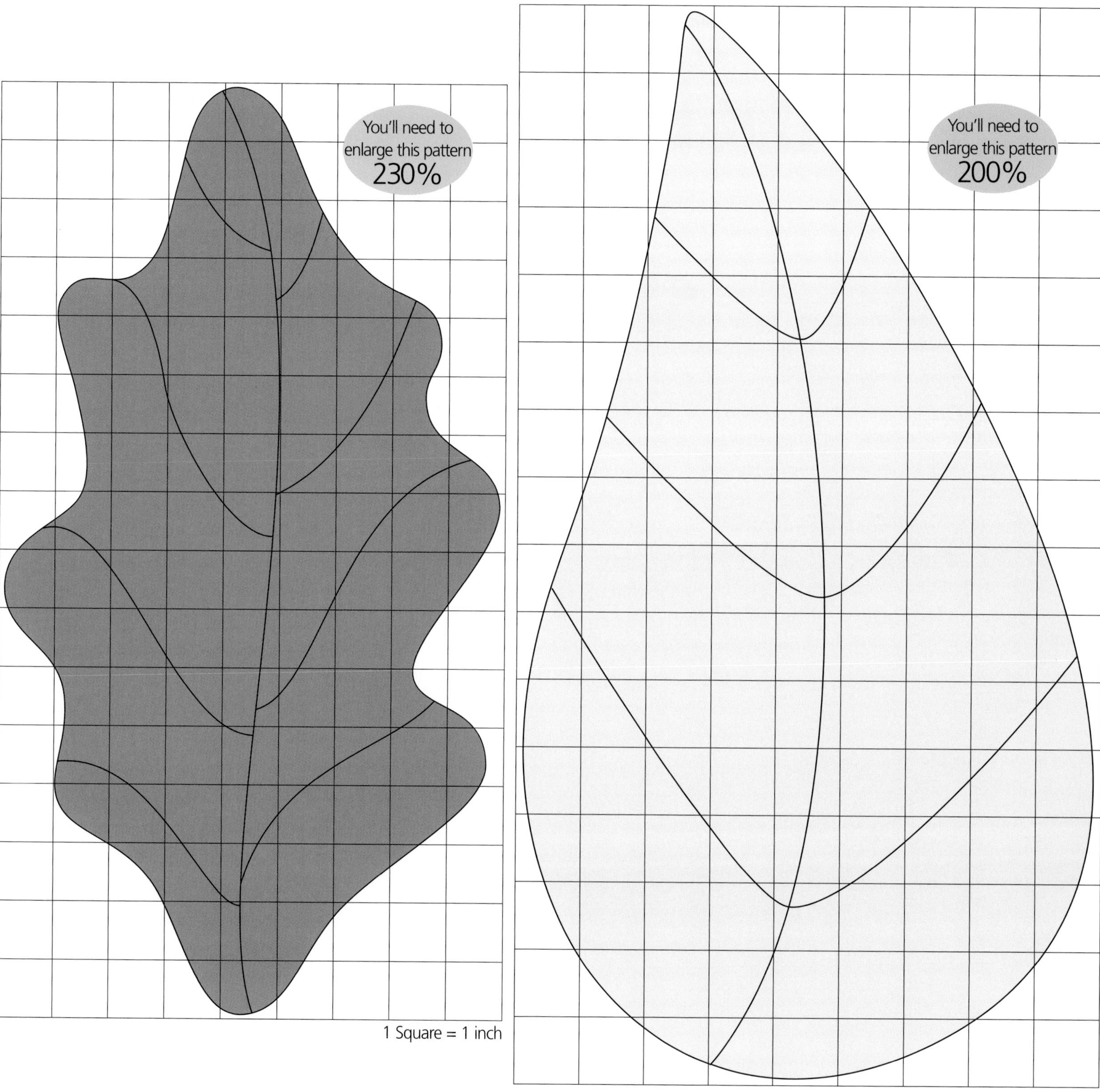
You'll need to enlarge this pattern 230%
1 Square = 1 inch
You'll need to enlarge this pattern 200%
1 Square = 1 inch

leaf-laden pots

Perfect for birthday gifts, these terra-cotta pots shimmer with vivid colors of spray paint.

To make a pot you will need:

Leaves
Heavy book, if needed
Terra-cotta flower pot and base
Gold enamel spray paint
Rubber cement
Burgundy, purple, or other desired colors of spray paint

1 **Choose leaves with interesting shapes** that will fit on the terra-cotta pot. To flatten leaves, place them under a heavy book until they become flat.

2 **Wash and dry the flower pot and base.** Spray two light and even coats of gold spray enamel on the outside and inside of the pot and the base. Let the paint dry.

3 **Brush rubber cement** on one side of the leaves. Let it dry. Brush on a second coat. Let it dry to a tacky, but not wet, stage. Position leaves onto the pot to create a pattern.

4 **Spray a light coat** of the desired paint color over the entire pot. Spray a second light coat if necessary. Let the paint dry.

5 **Peel off the leaves.** Rub off any remaining rubber cement from the pot.

1 more idea...

- Use holly leaves and berries to decorate pots for poinsettias at Christmastime.

also try this...

- In the summer, place citronella pillar candles in the pots or bases for your porch, deck, or patio.

more ideas *for* fall

- To collect a variety of autumn nature finds, write or call family and friends in other parts of the country to gather items for you.

- For last-minute Halloween gift sacks, place ghoulish stickers on lunch bags.

- Gather cattails to fill a large basket. Store upside down in a cool place until ready to use.

- To make a quick wreath, tie sprigs of bittersweet to a grapevine wreath using a variety of plaid ribbons.

- For an interesting centerpiece, paint several acorns with autumn colors to display in a bowl.

- Decoupage fallen leaves on a foam ball and wrap with jute or wire. Display on candleholders.

- Paint interesting-shape gourds using copper and gold metallic paints to display along a walkway for an unexpected treat.

- Let a child help you make your favorite pumpkin recipe.

- Carve pumpkins for Halloween using family members' faces as inspiration for the designs.

- Watch for preseason sales for holiday lighting and other decorations.

- Pin leaf charms, available at crafts stores, around the rim of a pillar candle.

- Visit a local crafts store to gather new supplies for outdoor fall decorating.

No one was ever great without some portion of divine inspiration.

— CICERO

winter

T*he chilling days of winter* are warmed by the kindness and sharing we show one another. Share your talents by creating this chapter's projects to give with the season's heartfelt sentiments.

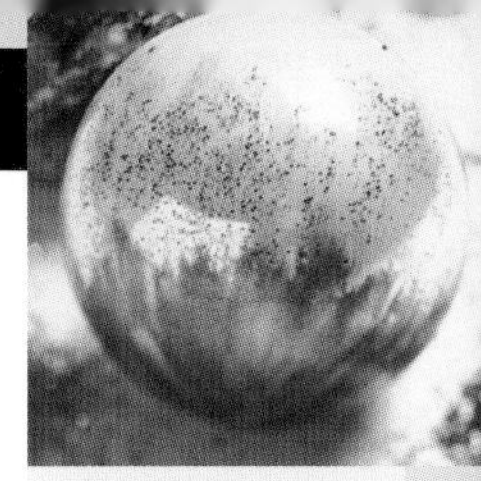

polished ornaments

Plain Christmas balls are given a radiant coating of color with strokes of fingernail polish.

To make an ornament you will need:
Glass ball ornament in desired color
Plain or glitter fingernail polish in desired color

here's how **To make this project,** decide what design to make on the ornament. Paint stripes, dots, swirls, or any other design you like.

Use the brush included with the fingernail polish to paint the ornament. The polish may pull off some of the original color of the ornament. This will create an interesting look, revealing the silver beneath. Cover the entire ornament with fingernail polish strokes or simply add random designs. Paint the bottom of the ornament and let dry. Paint the top. Let dry.

1 more idea...

- For a snow-capped ornament, paint it with white glitter fingernail polish.

also try this...

- Glue gems over the painted areas of the ornament for extra sparkle.

pinecone tiebacks

Bring a touch of woodland beauty to your indoor decorating by fashioning these interesting curtain tiebacks from nature's offerings.

To make a pair of tiebacks you will need:

2 large pinecones
Gloss varathane spray
Ice pick
2 screw eyes
24 inches of narrow gold wire-edged ribbon
1½ yards of gold cord
Hot-glue gun and hot-glue sticks
Small pinecones, dried pods, leaves, or other natural small items to embellish tops of large pinecones

here's how **To make this project,** spray the pinecones with varathane and allow to dry.

Use an ice pick to poke a hole in the top of each large pinecone. Insert a screw eye into the hole and twist into the pinecone to secure.

Slip a 12-inch piece of ribbon through the screw eye. Tie a knot at one end of the cord. Before tightening the knot, slip one end of the ribbon through the knot and tie the ribbon tightly around the knot, pulling the knot next to the screw eye. Repeat the process to attach the second pinecone to the other end of the cord.

Use hot glue to glue the knots to the top of the pinecones. Add other pinecones, leaves, pods, etc., to the top of the pinecones with glue.

1 more idea...

- For autumn gifts, make smaller versions of these ties to use for package embellishments.

also try this...

- Transform these tiebacks into holiday decorations by adding miniature Christmas balls, holly sprigs, or jingle bells.

beaded star ornament

Inspired by an antique trim, this exquisite star will add a touch of bygone days to your evergreen.

To make the ornament you will need:

- Medium-gauge crafts wire
- Silver beads
- Gold beads
- Star-shape cookie cutter
- Fine-gauge crafts wire
- Assorted small gold beads
- Six colored bugle beads
- One 5mm red bead
- ⅛-inch ribbon
- Small bell

here's how

To make this project, thread a 16-inch piece of medium-gauge wire with silver beads and a 12-inch piece of the wire with gold beads. For the silver strand, form around a star-shape cookie cutter. Add or delete beads to complete the shape. Twist the wire ends together on both beaded strands.

Bend the gold bead strand to form a circle around the star with points of the star touching the inside of the circle. Wire the top star point to the circle. Using fine-gauge wire, secure each bottom point of the star to the circle, leaving 4-inch-long wire tails.

String two bugle beads and then 7 to 10 small gold beads in the desired pattern onto each wire. Bring the wires together and thread a red bead over both wires.

Separate the wires again; string the remaining gold and bugle beads in the established pattern on each wire until only ½ inch of unbeaded wire remains. Bend wire ends up and poke them back through the second bead from bottom to secure in place.

Tie a ribbon bow at the top point. Add a small bell and loop for hanging if desired.

1 more idea...

- Make several of these trims to hang from greenery on a mantel.

also try this...

- Make Valentine trims by threading red beads on wire and forming around a heart-shape cookie cutter.

sweet treat jar

Keep holiday candies close at hand in a flea-market jar painted with three colors of the season.

To make a jar you will need:
Glass candy jar with lid and ball knob
Glass paints in maroon, white, dark green, and medium green
Disposable foam plate
Paintbrushes

1 **Wash and dry the candy** jar and lid. Avoid touching the areas to be painted.

2 **Place a small amount** of dark green, medium green, and white paint on a foam plate. Load a small flat paintbrush with all three colors of paint without mixing them. Paint two holly leaf shapes, *left*, on the lid of the jar.

3 **Load a small, pointed paintbrush** with dark green and white. Paint vein lines and outlines on each holly leaf. Let the paint dry.

4 **Place a small amount of maroon and white paint** on a foam plate. Load a flat brush and paint the knob on the jar lid. Let the paint dry.

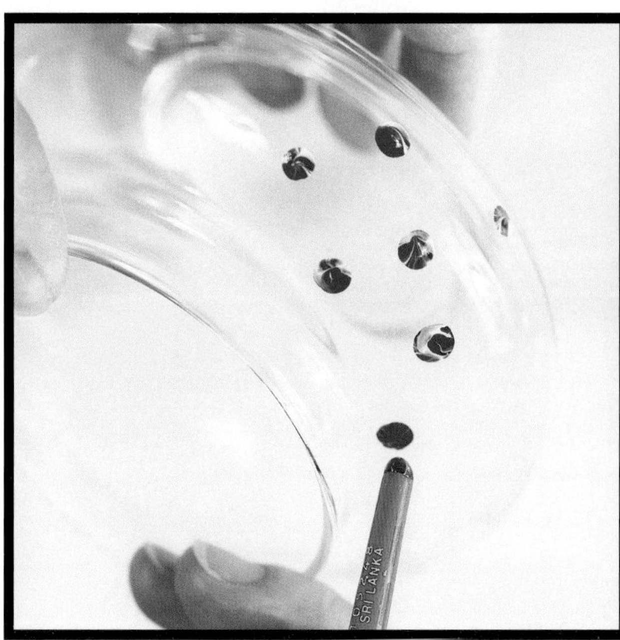

5 **To create the dots** on the jar base, dip the handle end of a paintbrush into the white and maroon paints and dot on the surface. Let the paint dry. Paint white dots on the jar lid around the holly designs. Let the paint dry.

1 more idea...

- Use this same idea to paint a holiday cookie jar or canister.

also try this...

- To give a jar as a gift, attach a tag to a ribbon and tie it around the lip of the jar.

frosted vase

White-as-snow wax lends a wintry touch to an otherwise ordinary clear glass vase.

To make a vase you will need:
Glass vase
White candles or white candle wax (available at crafts stores)
Clean metal can
Saucepan
Waxed paper
Spoon

1 **Fill the glass vase** with hot water to warm the glass.

2 **Cut candles into chunks** and remove the wick. Place the wax chunks into the metal can. Place the can into a saucepan of hot water on stove or electric burner. Heat until the wax melts. Carefully remove the can from the water. Never put wax directly in saucepan.

3 **Cover the work area** with waxed paper. Empty the water from the vase and dry it. Use a spoon to drizzle melted wax over the vase. Allow the wax to harden.

1 more idea...

- For other holidays, use colorful candles to achieve a look that's perfect for the season.

also try this...

- Apply melted wax to a shallow fish bowl and float candles inside for a dramatic effect.

good ideas *clever candy holders*

Mismatched glass candleholders—

upright, upside down, or stacked—make lovely serving pedestals for Christmas candies. Vary the designs and heights for interest, and group clear candleholders with small plates or saucers for an attractive holiday centerpiece.

festive package trims

Make the gift wrap as special as the gift by topping packages with these creative bows and tags that are made quick as a wink.

To make a bow you will need:

- Two 4-inch pieces of ¼-inch dowel
- Floral oasis
- Ribbon
- Scissors
- Trim for center of bow, such as a small toy, jingle bells, or plastic fruit
- Hot-glue gun and hot-glue sticks, or fine-gauge wire
- Paper
- Paper punch
- Cording, if desired

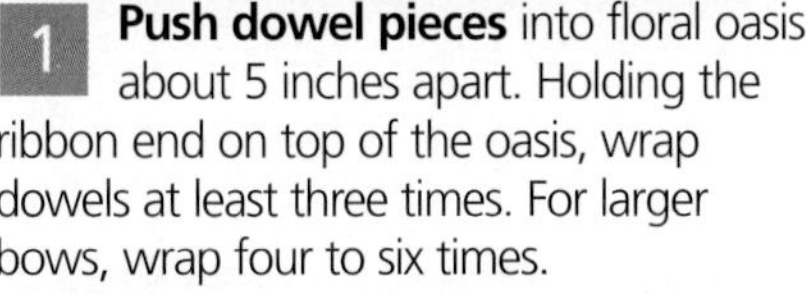

1 **Push dowel pieces** into floral oasis about 5 inches apart. Holding the ribbon end on top of the oasis, wrap dowels at least three times. For larger bows, wrap four to six times.

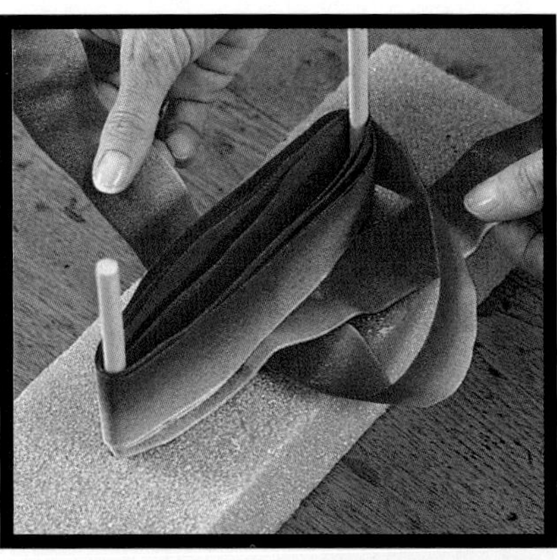

2 **Cut the ribbon,** leaving about an 8-inch tail. Slip tail of ribbon underneath loops, continuing to hold the starting end of the ribbon.

3 **Secure the loops** by tying the ribbon ends firmly into a knot in the center of the loops. Carefully slide the bow loops off the dowels.

4 **Tie the bow atop** intersecting ribbons that wrap around the package. Separate and fluff the loops. Fold ribbon ends in half and trim on the diagonal. If desired, glue or wire a trim to the center of the bow.

5 **For tag, cut a small paper piece** to fit on a section of ribbon as shown in the photograph, *opposite*. Glue the paper tag atop the ribbon. Insert the tag under the bow or punch a hole and add cording to tie it onto the package.

1 more idea...

- For extra-special center trims, use coins or wrapped candies.

also try this...

- Make several bows to trim a tree or to tuck among greenery on a banister or mantel.

season's greetings coasters

Two favorite symbols at Christmastime are permanently etched in glass on these stunning holiday coasters.

To make the coasters you will need:

Tracing paper
Pencil
Self-adhesive vinyl, such as Con-Tact paper
Scissors
Crafts knife
4-inch squares of ¼-inch thick glass with sanded edges
White vinegar
Spoon
Etching cream
Black permanent marking pen
White glass paint, such as Liquitex Glossies
Small paintbrush
Clear flat marbles or clear adhesive rubber bumper dots
Glass cement

1 **Trace the patterns,** *pages 76–77*, onto tracing paper. (In addition to the two designs shown *opposite*, we've included four other holiday motifs.) Cut the vinyl into 4-inch squares. Transfer the design to the back of the vinyl. Use a crafts knife to cut out the design.

2 **Clean each piece of glass** with water and white vinegar. Dry thoroughly. Remove the backing from the vinyl design and place on top of the glass. Rub the back with a spoon to remove the air bubbles.

3 **Apply etching cream** according to the manufacturer's directions. Wash off the cream and remove vinyl. Dry thoroughly.

4 **For reindeer, add eyes** using black marking pen. For the tree, paint on small white dots on the nonetched side of the coaster.

5 **Use cement to apply** a flat marble to each corner of the glass, or use adhesive bumpers.

1 more idea...

- Stack a set of coasters and tie with ribbon to give to a hostess.

also try this...

- Look for flat glass ornament shapes in crafts stores to make tree trims using the same technique.

season's greetings coasters (continued)

glittering goblets

Embellish a pretty goblet with glitter and float a candle in colored water for a sparkling effect.

To make the goblet you will need:
Clear crystal goblet
White crafts glue
Small bowl or dish
Gold glitter
Food coloring
Floating candles

here's how **To make this project,** wash and dry goblet. Carefully cover the rim of the goblet with glue. Fill a small bowl or dish with glitter. Press the goblet rim into the glitter. Let the glue dry.

Fill the goblet with colored water. Float a candle in the water. Sprinkle on more glitter for added sparkle.

1 more idea...

- Group several mismatched goblets and vary water colors for a breathtaking display.

also try this...

- For a large centerpiece, float several candles in a punch bowl. Surround with a wreath, if desired.

shimmering shakers

Inexpensive salt and pepper shakers become pieces of art when trimmed with tiny rhinestones.

To make the shakers you will need:

Glass salt and pepper shakers
Glass stain in red and turquoise, or etching cream
Glass cement
Tweezers
3mm rhinestones
Liquid gold pen with thin tip
¼-inch-wide masking tape

here's how **To make this project,** wash shakers. Let them dry. For the painted shakers, diagonally divide each side of shaker in half and paint the bottom half with glass stain. Paint each shaker a different color, if desired. Let dry. Use tweezers to pick up rhinestones, dip into cement, and evenly space along the diagonal edge of stain as desired. Let dry. Use gold pen to draw wiggly lines down from the edge of the rhinestones to the the bottom of the shaker.

For the etched shakers, wrap a length of masking tape at an angle around shaker. Burnish the edges of tape with fingernail. Etch top half of shaker with etching cream, following the manufacturer's directions. Wash off the etching cream and let dry. Cement rhinestones randomly over the etched area.

1 more idea...

- Add pizzazz to goblets, candleholders, vases, and other glass objects using this technique.

also try this...

- To add rhinestones temporarily to shakers, use dots of paint pen and peel off later.

bookmark ornaments

Ready to mark the pages of your favorite Christmas story or deck the branches of your Christmas tree, these bookmark beauties do double duty.

To make a bookmark you will need:

6-inch length of 2⅜-inch-wide 14-count Aida banding
Cotton embroidery floss in colors listed in key
Needle
2½ inches of ¾-inch-wide flat lace
Fabric glue
1×2-inch piece of paper-backed iron-on adhesive
2-yard strand of embroidery floss

here's how **To make this project,** tape or zigzag the edges of the Aida banding. Locate the center of the desired chart and the center of the banding; begin stitching there. Use three plies of embroidery floss to work cross-stitches. Work backstitches using two plies of floss.

Glue the lace trim to the bottom edge of the bookmark, securing the cut end on the back. Following the manufacturer's instructions, iron the adhesive to the wrong side of the bookmark above the design. Remove the paper backing and fold the top corners down to the center at a 45-degree angle to create a point as shown on the pattern on *page 81*. Fuse in place.

Poke a hole in the top of the bookmark ¼ inch from the point. Cut the 2-yard embroidery floss length in half. Twist the strand together. Fold the twisted strand in half; twist again to make a cord. Loop the cord through the hole and knot. Tie the ends together and trim.

1 more idea...

- Stitch the designs on 8-count fabric to make larger wall hangings.

also try this...

- Repeat a pattern across a shirt pocket, apron, or sweatshirt.

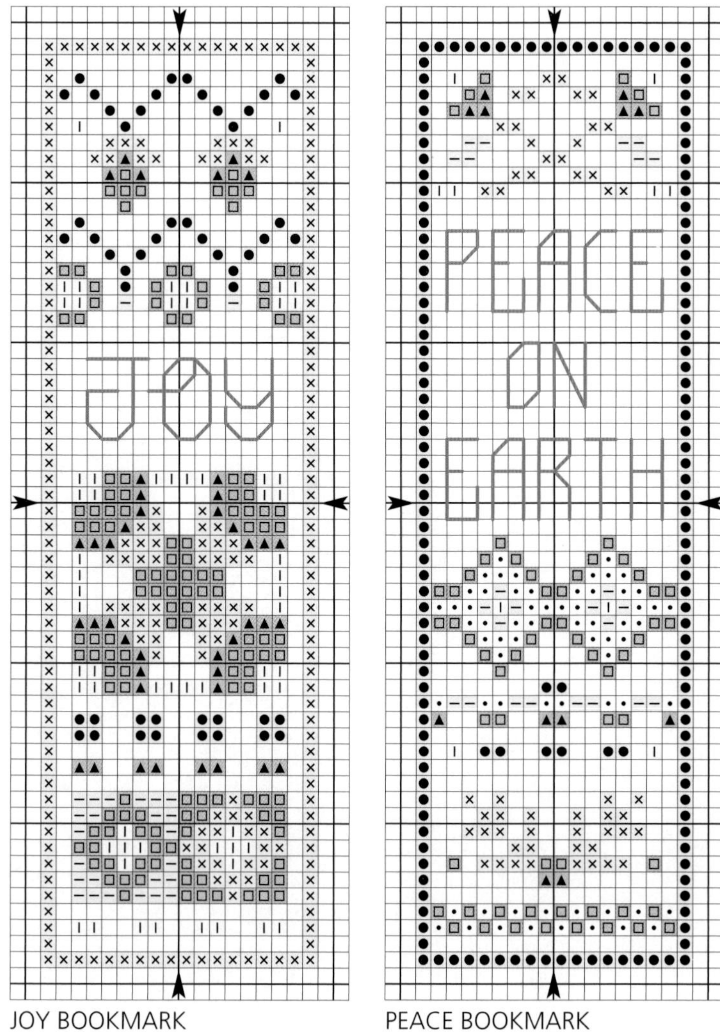

JOY BOOKMARK

PEACE BOOKMARK

BOOKMARK ORNAMENTS

ANCHOR	DMC
002	000 White
9046	321 True Christmas red
1005	498 Dark Christmas red
305	725 Topaz
230	909 Dark emerald
205	911 Medium emerald
204	913 Nile green
BACKSTITCH	
230	909 Dark emerald – all backstitches (2X)

Stitch count: 58 high x 18 wide

Finished design sizes:
14-count fabric – 4 x 1 inches
11-count fabric – 5 x 1 inches
18-count fabric – 3 x 1 inches

BOOKMARK ORNAMENTS PATTERN

musical wreath

Celebrate the sounds of the holidays with this gilded wreath that's just as lovely as the music itself.

To make the wreath you will need:
- Newspapers
- Gold spray paint
- Wire wreath form
- Gold glitter
- Chenille stems
- Thick white crafts glue
- Coarse brush
- Hot-glue gun and hot-glue sticks
- 36-inch piece of wired gold beads
- Ribbon

here's how **To make this project,** lay newspapers on work surface in a well-ventilated area. Spray wreath form with gold spray paint. While wet, sprinkle gold glitter on the wreath frame. Let it dry.

Using the photograph for ideas, shape musical notes and symbols from chenille stems. Coat the shapes with crafts glue. Use a coarse brush to spread the glue. Dip the shapes into gold glitter. Let dry.

Bend the glittered shapes to fit the wreath form. Hot-glue the shapes in place. Tie a ribbon bow to the top of the wreath. Add a gold bead bow atop the ribbon bow and coil the ends.

1 more idea...
- Make a musical garland for your tree by connecting the symbols with gold cord.

also try this...
- Shape chenille stems into coils and zigzags and cover with colorful glitter for a more contemporary look.

toasting goblets

Make an unforgettable toast to the season with these classy wire-wrapped glasses.

To make a goblet you will need:
Lead-free solder
Plastic-coated colored wire
Jingle bells
Clear glass goblet

here's how **To make this project** cut a piece of solder approximately 20 inches long. Wrap the solder piece with colored wire, letting the solder show through. If desired, wire on jingle bells while wrapping the solder.

Using the photograph for inspiration, begin wrapping the wire-wrapped solder around the goblet. Twist the ends into spirals if desired.

1 more idea...

- To give a bottle of champagne, wine, or sparkling cider, wrap the bottle neck with solder and colored wire.

also try this...

- Replace jingle bells with charms, beads, or ornate shank buttons.

good ideas *gilded ornaments*

Holiday ornaments in rich jewel tones become one-of-a-kind originals when touched with gold. To create the gilded designs, use a permanent metallic gold marking pen to make swirls, squiggles, or other decorative marks. Sign your work of art using a fine-line marking pen.

decorative die-cut cards

Recycle last year's Christmas cards, using their festive patterns to fill the tree and poinsettia cutouts.

To make a card you will need:
- Tracing paper
- Pencil
- Crafts knife
- Cutting mat
- White card with envelope
- Small paper punch
- Old Christmas cards
- Scissors
- Tape
- Heavy white paper
- Glue stick

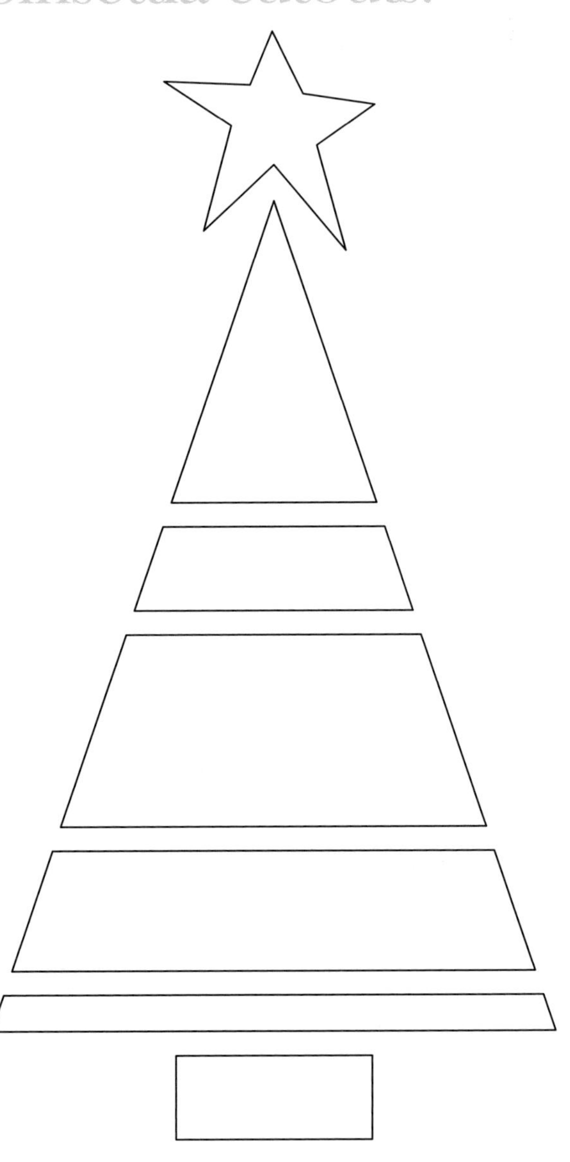

here's how **To make this project,** trace the desired pattern onto tracing paper. Lay the tracing paper on a cutting mat and cut out shapes from background using a crafts knife, leaving background piece intact.

Lay pattern over the front of the card and trace inside the pattern. Open the card, lay on the cutting mat, and cut out the shapes from the background. The dots in the center of the poinsettia are created using a small paper punch. Be sure to place the design where the paper punch will reach the flower center.

Use the pattern to trace shapes onto patterned portions of old Christmas cards. Cut out small shapes ⅛ inch beyond traced line. For the poinsettia, cut one piece for the center of the flower. The petals also can be created from one cut piece.

Tape the card pieces behind the cutout shapes. Cut a piece of paper slightly smaller than the card front. Glue paper piece over the taped card pieces. Let the glue dry.

1 more idea...
- Use the poinsettia and tree patterns as stencils for painting projects.

also try this...
- Add a small design to the envelope flap using the same technique.

christmas music caddy

Keep Christmas music organized in this decoupaged box that jingles all the way.

To make the compact disc caddy you will need:

- Black and white photocopies of old Christmas sheet music
- Decorative-edge scissors
- Decoupage medium
- Paintbrush
- Wood compact disc holder
- ¼-inch red cord
- Hot-glue gun and hot-glue sticks
- Medium-gauge silver wire
- 2 medium silver jingle bells
- 4 large silver jingle bells

1 **Trim the photocopies** of sheet music using decorative-edge scissors. Decide arrangement of sheet music on CD holder, trimming sheet music as needed.

2 **To apply sheet music to box,** paint the back of the music with decoupage medium. Position on box and paint the front with decoupage medium as shown, *left*. Be sure the top edge of the box is covered with sheet music. Continue adding pieces in this manner until the entire box is covered with sheet music. Let dry and paint on an additional coat of decoupage medium. Let dry.

3 **Measure the top edges of the box.** Add 10 inches to the measurement and cut cord to this length. Glue cord around the top edges of the box, leaving equal tails at one corner. Knot cord at corner and glue in place.

4 **Cut two 10-inch pieces of wire.** Thread a medium jingle bell on each piece of wire. Twist once to secure the jingle bell in the center of the wire. Tightly wrap the wires around the ends of the cord.

5 **Glue a large jingle bell** in each corner of the box bottom. Let dry.

1 more idea...

- To store children's music, cover the box with photocopies of old nursery rhymes and use wood blocks for the legs.

also try this...

- Make a larger version of this box to hold Christmas cards.

make it in minutes

gilded potpourri box

Freshen the air by filling this golden potpourri box with fragrant holiday scents.

To make the potpourri box you will need:

Tracing paper
Pencil
Scissors
5-inch-square thin cardboard box with separate lid
Small piece of tile
Utility knife with #11 blade
Paper
Ruler
Gold spray paint
Glitter gold paint pen
1 foot cloth window screen
Thick white crafts glue
Pearls on a string

here's how **To make this project,** center and trace the pattern on a piece of tracing paper that is cut the same size as the top of the lid.

Place tracing paper pattern on top of the box lid, pencil side down, and retrace over the back of the design. This will transfer the design to the lid. Remove the pattern.

Place the lid on a piece of tile and use a utility knife to cut out the design. The tile will allow the knife to glide.

Cut a 2-inch-square piece of paper for the diamond pattern on the sides of the box. Center the pattern on each side, ½ inch up from the bottom edge, and trace around the pattern. Use utility knife and a ruler to cut out the diamonds.

Spray the box and lid with gold spray paint. Use glitter gold paint pen to outline the lid design with dots.

Cut a 5-inch-square piece of window screen and glue to the inside of the lid. Cut and glue a 3-inch square of screen to the inside, behind each of the diamond cutouts.

Glue a row of pearls around the outside edge of the lid and another row of pearls around the bottom edge of the side of the lid. Glue a row of pearls around the diamond shapes on all four sides of the box.

1 more idea...

- Present wrapped candies or baked goods in these beautiful gift containers.

also try this...

- Replace the screen with colorful cellophane if using for a gift box.

christmas tassels

Dangle these whimsical tassels from a coat hook, over a doorknob, or on your Christmas tree for a playful touch in your holiday home.

1 **Using the photograph,** *opposite,* for ideas, paint the wood finial. Let the paint dry between colors. To add dots, dip the handle end of the paintbrush into paint and dot onto the surface. Let dry. To make stripes, use a fine liner brush. Let dry. Drill a small hole in the top of the finial.

2 **Cut pieces from knit fabric,** a 4×18-inch piece for the small tassel and a 6×24-inch piece for the large tassel. Machine-baste ½ inch from one long edge.

3 **Fold the fabric in half** lengthwise. Use scissors to cut straight fringes approximately ¼ inch wide as shown, *left*, stopping short of the basting stitches.

4 **Place a line of glue** at one end of fabric between the basting stitches and the edge. Roll the fabric around the bottom of the finial as shown, *left.* Do not stretch fabric. Continue gluing fabric around finial. Let dry.

5 **Cut a short piece of fringed trim** to fit over fabric. Glue in place. Let dry.

6 **Glue rhinestones and beads** on finial and fringe as desired. Let dry.

7 **Cut a 7-inch piece** of cord. Glue the ends in the hole in the finial. Slip a bead over loop if desired.

To make a tassel you will need:

Wood finial
Acrylic paints in turquoise, pink, black, ocher, and lavender, or other desired colors
Paintbrush
Drill with small bit
Knit fabric
Scissors
Tape measure
Thread
Thick white crafts glue
Fringed trim
Rhinestones
Bugle beads
Thin cord
Round bead, if desired

1 more idea...

- Secure two coordinating tassels to the ends of heavy cording to make a curtain tieback.

also try this...

- For a shortcut, use purchased fringe trim instead of cutting knit fabric for the tassel.

good ideas *give them gold boxes*

Purchased white boxes become dazzling gift containers when you add simple designs in gold rickrack. Use these boxes for inspiration to make your own. Use small dabs of crafts glue to hold the rickrack in place.

winter white wreath

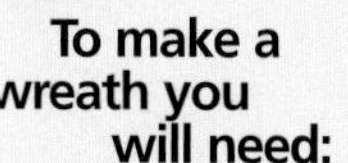

Greet your guests with a welcoming wreath made from a ring of tapioca and glistening jewels.

1 **If using a foam disk, use a can to cut the center circle.** Smooth the edges of the wreath shape by pressing firmly with your fingers.

2 **Coat the entire top surface** and edges with a generous coat of crafts glue. Place the tapioca onto the glued surfaces. Let dry. It may take several hours or overnight to dry.

3 **Paint two coats** of white paint over the tapioca. Let the paint dry.

4 **Cut a round circle** from white cardboard, approximately $3\frac{3}{4}$ inches in diameter. Outline the edge of the circle with a generous amount of crafts glue. Place a decorative cord or braid trim around the edge. Trim off any excess. Let dry.

5 **Spread a generous amount** of crafts glue on the cardboard circle. Arrange the jewelry pieces as you wish in the circle. Arrange the largest pieces first, *left,* filling in the small areas. If there are tiny areas to fill, sprinkle on glitter and tiny beads and shells.

6 **Tie a bow from wide gold** wire-edged ribbon. Hot-glue it to the center of the wreath. When the medallion is dry and jewels firmly in place, hot-glue the medallion to the center of the bow.

7 **To apply a hook on the back,** first create a firm, smooth surface. Using a smooth piece of cardboard, glue it to the back with Liquid Nails adhesive. Glue a metal hook to the cardboard. Allow to dry overnight.

To make a wreath you will need:

- 10-inch-diameter foam disk or a foam wreath form, such as Styrofoam
- Metal can, approximately 4 inches in diameter, if needed
- Thick white crafts glue
- Large tapioca
- White acrylic paint
- Paintbrush
- $3\frac{1}{4}$-inch-diameter white cardboard circle
- Scissors
- 12-inch piece of cord or braid
- Jewelry pieces in pastel colors
- Small beads and shells
- Glitter
- Several $\frac{1}{2}$-inch-diameter gold beads
- 30 inches of wide gold wire-edged ribbon
- Hot-glue gun and hot-glue sticks
- Metal hanger
- Small piece of cardboard about 2 inches square
- Strong adhesive, such as Liquid Nails

1 more idea...

- Jeweled bows make elegant tree toppers.

also try this...

- Simplify the medallion to craft special bows for holiday packages.

star-struck cookie plate

Leave Santa cookies on this colorfully painted plate, and he will leave something special in your stocking.

To make the plate you will need:

Tracing paper
Pencil with round-tip eraser
Tape
Clear glass plate
Permanent black marker
Glass paints in yellow, purple, green, red, white, and black
Paintbrush

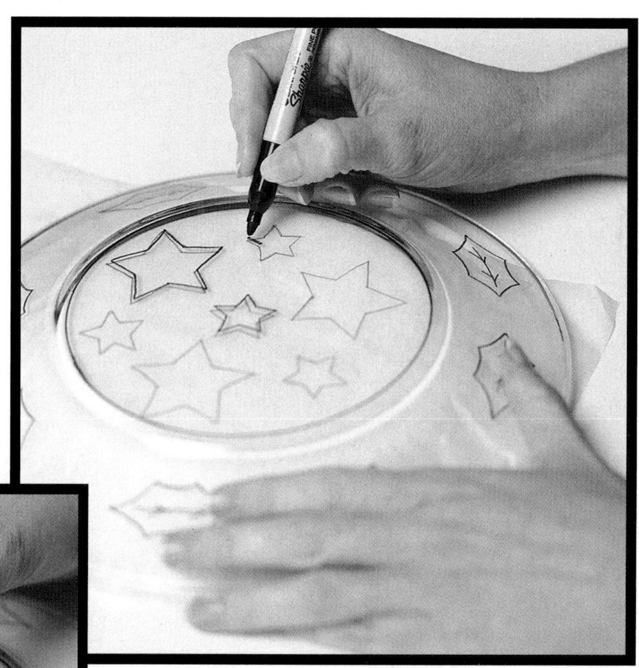

1 **Trace the star** and holly patterns as many times as desired onto tracing paper. Tape the patterns in place with right side onto top plate surface so the pattern shows through to the back of plate. You will do all work on the back side.

2 **Trace the outlines** of the patterns, *below,* with a black permanent marker. Draw in veins of holly leaves.

3 **Paint inside pattern shapes** first, painting the stars and holly as shown, *left*. Add berry dots by dipping a pencil eraser into red paint and making three dots on the surface. Add white dots. Let the paint dry. Look at the front side of the plate to see if it looks as you wish, making sure paint is covering well and is not transparent.

4 **Paint over the circled star area** with purple paint. Paint over the yellow stars. Paint the black area next, covering the holly and white dots. Let dry.

5 **Paint the red checks next** using a small flat brush. When dry, paint over the border with white. Let paint dry for 24 hours and bake in oven if directed by paint manufacturer.

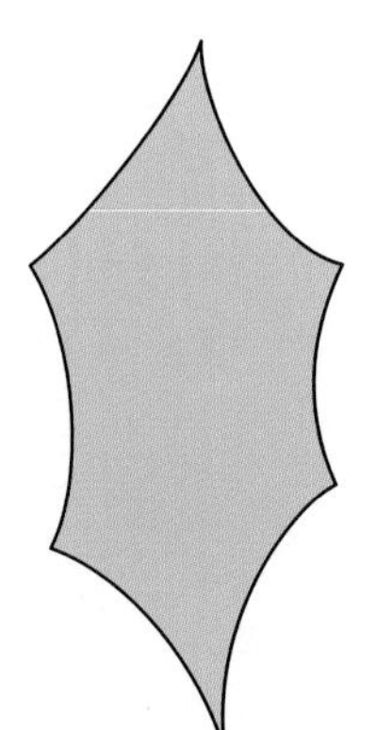

1 more idea...

- Teach children this technique so they can make gifts for teachers and grandparents.

also try this...

- To make other motifs, trace cookie cutters or use designs from simple coloring books.

glorious gift bags

Gifts of their own, these easy-sew bags have cording ties to keep contents safely inside.

To make a bag you will need:

Sheer or satin fabric (see instructions for amount)
Ruler
Pencil
Scissors
Needle and thread to match fabric
Grommets
Grommet punch and hammer
Decorative braid to fit through grommets
Tassels to match braid
Cotton embroidery floss to match braid
Needle
Waxed paper
Thick white crafts glue
Rhinestones
Metallic gold paint pen
Star studs

here's how **To make this project,** choose the size or sizes of bags you wish to make. For a bag appropriate to hold a wine bottle, begin with a piece of fabric 7½×16 inches. For a medium-size bag, begin with a piece of fabric 16×10 inches. For a small bag, start with a piece of fabric 12×7 inches. Cut the fabric to desired size.

Machine-stitch a ⅛-inch folded hem, wrong side under, along the top edge of the fabric.

Fold the piece of fabric in half, right side inward. Sew the side seam and the bottom seam. Trim off excess thread. Trim neatly and press seams open. Turn right side out. Press again.

Fold the top hemmed edge downward inside the bag to make about a 3-inch fold on the larger bags and a 1½-inch hem on the small bag. Press again, pressing the fold on top.

Using a grommet punch, apply grommets around the top edge in the top folded area of the bag. Add an odd number of grommets, such as 5, 7, or 9. Measure with a ruler and mark with a pencil first, before inserting grommets.

Insert braided trim into grommets, weaving in and out. String a long piece of embroidery floss onto a needle. Attach the tassels to each end of the braid. Sew on with embroidery floss and wrap around and around until well covered. Sew the end of the embroidery thread into the braid, securely hiding it in the braid.

Insert a piece of waxed paper inside the bag. Add small dots of glue randomly to the bag and apply rhinestones or make swirls with paint pen. Add star studs, if desired.

1 more idea...

- Hole-punch a gift tag to slip over one end before tying the cording into a bow.

also try this...

- Cover vases with these lovely bags to add a festive holiday touch.

jingle bell hat and gloves

Little girls will jingle jangle jingle while keeping toasty warm in this fun hat-and-gloves set.

To make the set you will need:

- 24 inches of 1-inch-wide plaid ribbon
- 4 jingle bells in each color: red, green, and blue
- Nylon sewing thread to match ribbon
- Purchased hat and gloves in desired colors
- Needle
- 1 yard of ¼-inch-wide plaid ribbon

here's how **To make the gloves,** cut the 1-inch-wide ribbon in half. Tie each piece into a bow. Sew one of each color of jingle bell in the center of each bow. Tack onto cuff of glove.

To make the hat, thread three jingle bells onto the ¼-inch-wide ribbon. Make three even loops in ribbon, sliding a jingle bell to the bottom of each loop. Sew the tops of the loops together and tack to the point of the hat. Sew remaining jingle bells to top of hat.

1 more idea...

- Use this same technique to trim a little girl's sweater.

also try this...

- To make a hair bow, sew a barrette to the back of the bow and bells.

plaid and polka-dot platter

Serve guests in holiday style with this festive glass tray that takes just minutes to paint.

To make the platter you will need:
- Glass platter with handles
- Disposable foam plate
- Glass paints in red, green, and white
- Paintbrushes
- Pencil with round-tip eraser

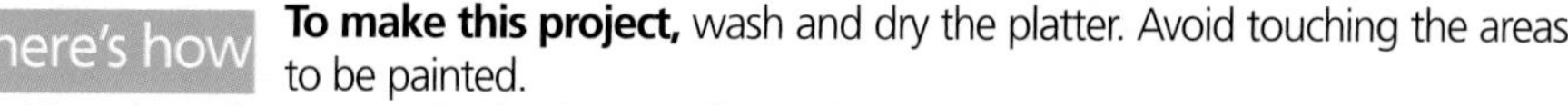

here's how **To make this project,** wash and dry the platter. Avoid touching the areas to be painted.

Place a small amount of red paint on a foam plate. Paint the handle areas of the platter red, leaving approximately ⅛ inch around the outer edges. To add large dots, dip the eraser end of a pencil into the red paint and dot evenly spaced around the platter edge. Let the red paint dry.

Use a ¼-inch flat paintbrush to add green stripes over the red paint on the handles. Use the photograph, *above*, as a guide. Add small green lines to the center of each red dot. Let dry.

To add white to the handle areas, use a fine-point paintbrush. Make a white + on each red area, filling the space as shown in the photograph. Cross the green lines in the red dots with white. Add small white dots around the platter edge by dipping the handle end of a paintbrush into paint and dotting on the surface. Let the paint dry.

If desired, turn the platter over and paint dots in the center of the platter. Let the paint dry. Do not paint areas that will come in contact with food.

Bake the platter in the oven if directed by the paint manufacturer.

1 more idea...
- Make matching dinnerware using clear glass plates, bowls, cups, and saucers.

also try this...
- Make a platter for each season by changing the colors of paint used.

make it in minutes

singing star ornaments

Old sheet music plays a starring role when transformed into stunning tree ornaments.

To make an ornament you will need:

Tracing paper
Pencil
Scissors
Lightweight cardboard
Photocopied page of old sheet music
Large sewing needle
Knitting needle or other scoring stylus
Ruler
Fine gold cord
6mm gold beads

here's how **To make this project,** trace desired size of star pattern, *left,* onto tracing paper and cut out. Draw around the pattern on cardboard, making a template. Cut out the cardboard star. Trace around template on photocopied sheet music as many times as desired. Cut out stars.

Poke a small hole in the center of the star using a needle. Referring to the pattern, use the scoring stylus and a ruler to score solid lines on the right side of the star. Turn the star over and score the broken lines.

Fold each point on the lines scored on front. Turn star over and fold on the lines scored on back.

Thread needle with fine gold cord. Pull through the tip of one star point. Remove the needle, and thread the ends of the cord through one or two gold beads. Knot the ends together to make a hanging loop.

1 more idea...

- Make a star garland by sewing the star tips together to form a line of stars.

also try this...

- Use the patterns to make stars from wrapping paper (backed by a heavier paper) or old Christmas cards.

good ideas *holiday swag*

A short stick makes a natural form for this quick-and-easy swag. Use floral wire to attach sprigs of greenery, small pinecones, and berries atop new or antique ornaments. Add bows to complete this welcoming Christmas decoration.

happy new year serving tray

When the clock strikes midnight, you'll be ready for the celebration with this classy clock tray, bright with metallic paints and a rainbow of colorful gems.

To make the tray you will need:
- Wood serving tray with deep sides
- Acrylic paints in black and metallic copper, turquoise, and purple
- Paintbrush
- Clock faces from flea-market finds
- Thick white crafts glue
- Acrylic gems in various sizes, shapes, and colors
- Silicone glue
- Gold leaf paint
- ¼-inch dowel
- Glass cut to fit inside tray

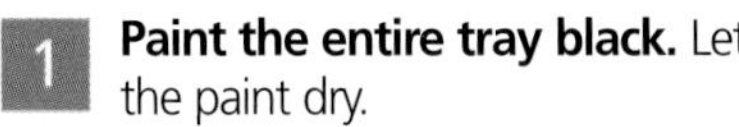

1 **Paint the entire tray black.** Let the paint dry.

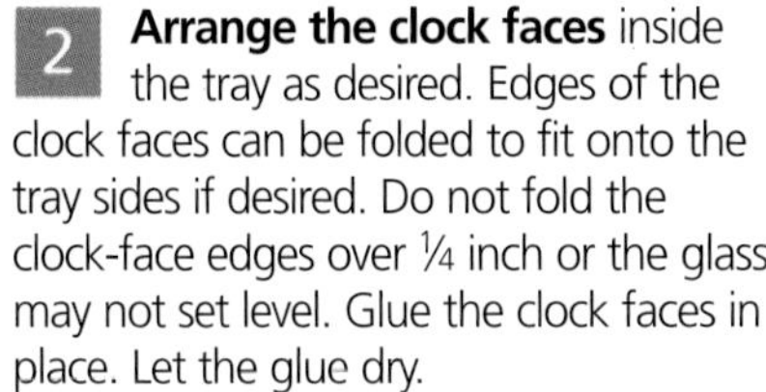

2 **Arrange the clock faces** inside the tray as desired. Edges of the clock faces can be folded to fit onto the tray sides if desired. Do not fold the clock-face edges over ¼ inch or the glass may not set level. Glue the clock faces in place. Let the glue dry.

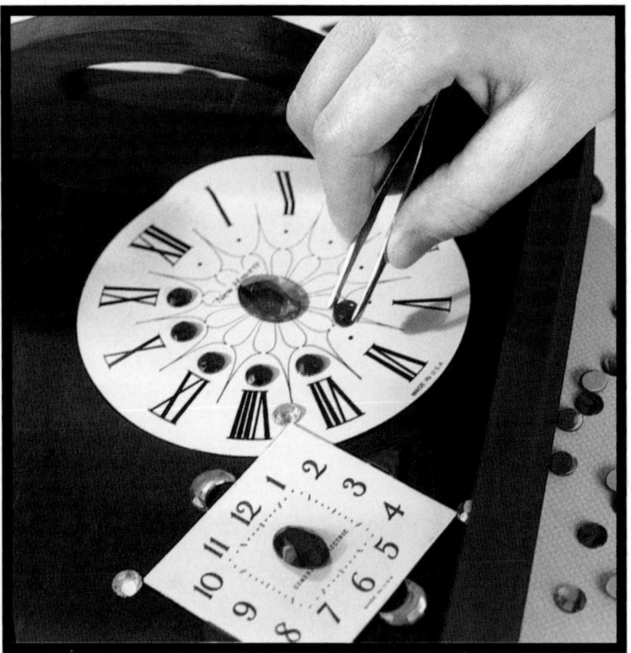

3 **Using the photograph for inspiration,** use tweezers and silicone glue to adhere gems on and around the clock faces. Let the glue dry.

4 **With very little paint on the brush,** dry-brush around the clock faces and gems using gold leaf paint as shown, *left.* Use straight brush strokes and a little copper paint to dry-brush the outside of the tray. Use turquoise for the top edge, and dry-brush the inside of the handles with purple. Let the paint dry.

5 **Cut four equal pieces of dowel** to raise the glass up, just below the handles. Paint the dowel pieces black. Let dry. Dry-brush with gold leaf. Let dry. Glue a dowel in each corner of the tray using silicone glue. Let dry.

6 **Clean the glass.** Glue the glass to the top of the dowels. Let dry. Add a gem in each corner of the glass. Let dry.

1 more idea...

- To use as decoration only, omit the glass and display the tray with several tabletop clocks set around it.

also try this...

- For a teen, embellish either a wall or tabletop clock using gems and metallic paints.

celebration glassware

Perfect for a party, or any time, these clear glass pieces make get-togethers a special event.

To make a piece of glassware you will need:
Clear glass candleholder
Glass paints in desired colors
Paintbrushes
Pencil with a round-tip eraser

here's how **To make this project,** wash and dry the glassware. Avoid touching the areas to be painted.

To paint the underside of a piece of glassware, such as the taper candleholder base, begin by painting the design. To make dots, dip the eraser end of a pencil or paintbrush handle into paint and dot onto the surface. Repeat as many times as desired. Let the paint dry. Paint on the background color.

To paint the outside of a piece of glassware, such as the votive holder rim, begin by painting the background color. Let it dry. Paint stripes and dots as desired. Let dry.

Bake in the oven to cure if directed by the paint manufacturer. Let cool in oven before handling.

1 more idea...

- For a coordinating tray, paint the glass of a picture frame and secure the backing with a piece of wood.

also try this...

- For temporary, peel-off glass decorating, use fabric paint pens.

let's-play snack trays

Perfect for a light snack while playing cards, these trays and cups win high scores with their striking colors.

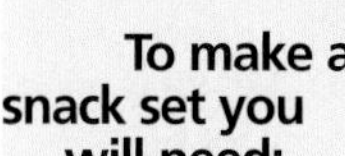

To make a snack set you will need:

Glass snack tray and cup
Glass paints in black, yellow, white, turquoise, red, pink, and lime green
Paintbrushes

here's how **To make this project,** wash and dry the glassware. Avoid touching the areas to be painted. Do not paint where food or drink will touch.

On this set, the underside of the tray edge was painted. Begin by painting stripes and dots as shown, using all colors except black. Let the paint dry. Paint over the design with black. Let the paint dry.

Paint the cup bottom in the same manner as the tray. Paint a stripe around the cup if the cup design allows. Let dry. Bake in the oven if directed by the paint manufacturer.

1 more idea...

- Change the look of each snack set by painting a different background color on each piece.

also try this...

- Paint the backside center of the tray, if the cut-glass design is smooth enough to paint.

make it in minutes

bow-topped valentine

Pretty enough to frame, this pastel Valentine card is sure to hold words from the heart.

To make a Valentine you will need:
Crocheted heart doily or piece of lace
Scissors
Heavy white card stock
Decoupage medium
Paintbrush
Pastel pink pearl acrylic paint
White ribbon
Pink ribbon rose
Thick white crafts glue

here's how **To make this project,** use a purchased crocheted heart or lace piece that can be cut into a heart shape.

Cut a piece of heavy white card stock double the size of the heart doily or pink pattern. Cut it larger than the heart shape and double the height. Fold the paper in half.

Position the lace heart onto folded paper, lining up top edges along the top fold. If using a lace piece, trace the heart pattern, *above*, and cut lace using the pattern. Paint decoupage medium over the crocheted heart, soaking through onto card stock and adhering the heart to the card. Allow to dry.

When decoupage medium is dry, paint with pink paint. Let the paint dry.

With the card folded, cut away the paper around the outer edge of heart. Cut through both layers of card stock.

Make a bow from white ribbon and glue to front of heart. Glue a small ribbon rose in the center of the bow.

1 more idea...

- Make a heart on a single layer of paper, mount on a background paper, and frame for an everlasting Valentine.

also try this...

- Sew a charm initial in the center of the heart to personalize it.

brushstroke platter

Make this dazzling platter at the last minute with quick strokes of metallic and white paints.

To make a platter you will need:
- Glass platter with some smooth areas cut into glass
- Glass paints in white and metallic copper, gold, and silver
- ¼-inch flat paintbrush

1 more idea...
- Make several coordinating serving pieces using this quick-paint process.

also try this...
- To speed up the process, use a hair dryer on low speed to help dry the paint quickly.

here's how **To make this project,** wash and dry glassware. Avoid touching areas to be painted. Do not paint where food will touch.

On this platter, the underside was painted. Begin by painting U-shape white brushstrokes as shown. Let the paint dry. Add silver, copper, and gold brushstrokes in the same manner, letting dry between coats.

Add a checkered border if desired. Let dry. Bake the piece in the oven if directed by the paint manufacturer.

starry night snowman

Full of joy, this miniature snowman admires a shining star from above.

To make the snowman and tree you will need:

White air-dry clay, such as Crayola Model Magic clay
2 toothpicks
Grommet
Small sticks for arms
Iridescent paint-on glitter
Enamel paints in orange, black, and metallic gold
Paintbrush
8-inch piece of ½-inch-wide silver ribbon
Scissors
4-inch cardboard star with flat side
Ice pick
8-inch stick
Thick white crafts glue
Beading wire
1½-inch silver star sequin
Clear seed bead

here's how **To make the snowman,** roll three small balls of clay the sizes of a grape, walnut, and golf ball. Form the two larger balls into ovals.

Break a toothpick in half. Use the toothpick pieces to hold the clay shapes together. Press the three pieces of clay firmly together. Press a grommet into the bottom piece of clay so the snowman will stand. Form a small carrot-shape nose and press onto face. Push a small stick in each side of the body for an arm. Let the clay dry.

Brush the snowman with paint-on glitter. Let dry. Paint the nose orange. Use the remaining toothpick to paint the mouth dots and lines for eyes. Let the paint dry. Paint glitter on the top of the nose. Let the paint-on glitter dry.

Tie the ribbon around the neck for a scarf. Trim the ends.

To make the tree, poke a small hole in the center top of the cardboard star base using an ice pick. Paint the star gold. Let dry. Glue the stick into the hole in the star. Let dry. Paint the stick and the star with glitter. Let dry.

Cut a 2-inch piece of wire. Thread through star sequin. Add a seed bead, return wire end through hole in sequin, and twist the wire ends to secure. Attach the wire end to one piece of the stick.

1 more idea...

- Make larger snowmen by forming clay around plastic foam balls and egg shapes.

also try this...

- Hang miniature ornaments on the limbs of the stick tree.

good ideas *heart hankie curtains*

Tie or stitch together new or vintage handkerchiefs to make a window covering as special as Valentine's Day. Use a single row of hankies for a valance, or make any size curtain you want.

from the heart vase

Remember someone special with a Valentine bouquet presented in a lovely vase that sparkles with gold accents.

To make a vase you will need:
Masking tape
Glass vase
Gold spray paint
Tracing paper
Pencil
Scissors
Glass paints in peach and white
Paintbrush
Gold glitter paint pen

1 **Use masking tape** to section off a rectangular area on the vase. Leave the rectangle uncovered and cover the rest of the bottle with tape. Spray the bottle with two or three light coats of gold spray paint, allowing to dry between coats. Let the paint dry. Carefully remove the tape.

2 **Trace the heart pattern,** *right,* onto tracing paper. Cut out the heart pattern and trace the shape onto the gold painted area.

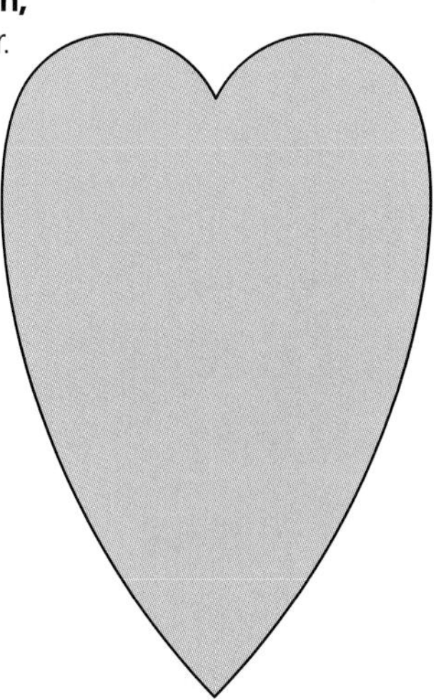

3 **Paint the heart** using peach paint. It may require two coats. Add peach dots in the gold area by dipping the handle end of the paintbrush into paint and dotting onto the surface. Add white dots inside the peach heart. Let the paint dry.

4 **Outline the heart** with gold glitter paint pen. Let it dry.

1 more idea...

- Make a framed piece in this manner by painting on the glass that comes with the frame.

also try this...

- Use paint pen to repeat the words "I love you" or an appropriate poem around the vase.

endearing valentines

Express heartfelt sentiments to your dear ones by sending these dainty heart cards.

To make the lavender valentine you will need:
White card stock
Scissors
Small crocheted heart doily
Decoupage medium
Paintbrush
Acrylic paints in white pearl and lavender pearl
Thick white crafts glue
Flat white pearl decorations

To make the peach valentine you will need:
White air-dry clay, such as Crayola Model Magic
Heart-shape cookie cutter
Scissors
Textured heavy paper
Thick white crafts glue
Card stock
Acrylic paint in white pearl and peach pearl
Paintbrush
Small gold beads

here's how **To make the lavender card with the large heart,** use a piece of small card stock slightly larger than the doily. Lay the doily on the paper and brush decoupage medium over it. Let it dry. Paint it with an acrylic white pearl paint. Let the paint dry. Trim off paper neatly and closely around the outer edge of the heart.

Make a folded card large enough to accommodate the doily on paper. Paint the front of card in lavender pearl. Let it dry. Glue the white heart onto the lavender card. Glue small flat pearl decorations in each corner of card.

here's how **To make the peach card,** roll out a small piece of clay to about ⅛ inch thick. Cut out small heart shape with cookie cutter. Let heart shape air-dry.

Cut out a small square from textured paper. Cut it larger than the heart. Glue heart onto paper square. Make card from card stock that is larger than square. Fold card stock in half so that the back half is about ⅛ inch wider than front. Paint card peach on front and white on inside.

Glue the square with the heart onto the center of the peach square. Glue a small gold bead in each corner of the white square. Let the glue dry.

1 more idea...

- Personalize the card by tacking an "I love you" charm in the center.

also try this...

- Add words or decorative details to the card using paint pen.

more ideas *for* winter

- Tie various lengths of fish line to plastic snowflakes and secure to the edges of the roof.
- Fill mix-and-match silver vases with greenery and red roses to adorn the mantel or buffet.
- Teach children the importance of showing appreciation by helping them make and write thank-you notes.
- Place a mirror on the mantel to reflect flickering candles.
- Tie a red-and-green plaid bow on the mailbox or gate.
- Use purchased red tassels on cording to tie up white linen napkins for a special night of entertaining.
- Play recorded holiday music while enjoying an evening of gift making.

- Plan a caroling night with friends.
- Wire together greens to create a wreath in an unusual shape, such as a square, diamond, or crescent moon.
- Visit flea markets and antiques shops for vintage holiday linens and trims.
- For a fun kitchen display, fill a large, clear cookie jar with holiday cookie cutters or colorful ornaments.
- Invite a child to help wrap Christmas gifts.
- Offer to do some holiday shopping for someone who is ill or housebound.
- Create your own Christmas wraps by stamping simple designs on brown kraft paper.

Heard melodies are sweet,
but those unheard are sweeter.

—JOHN KEATS

R*enew your spirit* with creations that mirror the lovely awakenings of spring. Brimming with color, these projects will be as fun and exciting as watching the blooms unfold in your garden.

spring

elegant wedding candle

Honor the happy bride and groom with a romantic wedding candle trimmed with rings of woven beads and roses.

To make the candle you will need:

- Large 3-wick candle
- Two woven bead bridal headbands (available at crafts stores)
- Small and medium artificial roses on wires

1 more idea...

- Embellish the candle even more by pinning pearl beads all over the candle.

also try this...

- Trim the wedding cake using fresh rose heads in the same colors as used on the candle.

here's how **To make this project,** wrap one beaded headband around the base of the candle. Twist the wire ends of the headband together to secure. Trim the excess. Wrap the second headband around the candle, approximately 1½ inches from the top. Secure in the same manner.

If necessary, separate the small wired roses. Trim the wires to about ¾ inch. Carefully push a wire into the candle, just below the top headband. Continue adding roses every 2 inches. Add the medium-size roses at the base, arranging 3 to 5 roses in a grouping.

baby photo holder

New snapshots or those from decades ago can be enjoyed by all when displayed in this whimsical baby block holder.

To make the holder you will need:

B, A, B, and Y baby blocks
Ice pick
Hammer
Hot-glue gun and hot-glue sticks
Needle-nose pliers
Four 18-gauge craft wires varying between 8 and 14 inches in length
⅝-inch wood dowel
Wire cutter

here's how **To make this project,** make a hole in the center top of each block using an ice pick and hammer.

Hot-glue the blocks together, placing the A and Y blocks ¼ inch behind the two B blocks. Let the glue dry.

Use needle-nose pliers to twist a small loop at one end of each wire. Wrap this end around the wood dowel twice. Slip off the dowel and use pliers to bend remaining length of wire down into a vertical stem.

Cut the wires at different lengths. Hot-glue the end of each wire into a hole in a block. Let the glue dry.

1 more idea...

- Spell congratulations with blocks and add appropriate photos for the occasion.

also try this...

- Give a photo holder as a baby shower gift, placing a gift certificate in it.

color burst seed balls

The vibrant hues of the season shine through in these fun decorations bursting with texture.

1 To cover a ball with small items, fill a paper plate with rice, beans, or seeds. Using a craft stick, coat one section of the foam ball at a time with a generous amount of glue. Roll the coated ball in the plate or use your fingers to place the items on the foam ball. Cover the entire ball.

2 To cover a foam ball with raffia spread glue randomly around ball. It does not have to be entirely covered. Begin wrapping around the ball in one direction. When an area is covered, continue wrapping in the opposite direction. Continue until the ball is completely covered. Use straight pins to hold the raffia in place until dry.

3 To cover the ball with leaves use semidry leaves, not too dry or brittle. Spread glue on back of leaves and press onto ball. Continue to glue and overlap the leaves until the ball is covered.

4 Paint each covered ball a different color using desired colors of paint. Using a medium-size flat paintbrush, paint with a generous amount of paint, working the paint into the crevices. Let dry.

5 Use a very small amount of gold paint on your fingertip. Gently rub gold over raised areas to create a highlight.

6 If desired, wrap balls with gold ribbon threaded with colored beads.

To make the seed balls you will need:

- 2½- to 3½-inch plastic foam balls, such as Styrofoam
- Rice, beans, leaves, sunflower seeds, and raffia
- Paper plate
- Craft stick
- Thick white crafts glue
- Straight pins
- Acrylic paints in hot pink, lavender, yellow, green, and orange
- Medium-size flat paintbrush
- Gold highlighting paint, such as Rub 'n' Buff
- Narrow gold ribbon
- Multicolored beads

1 more idea...

- For kids, try this technique using alphabet macaroni.

also try this...

- To hang these seeded creations, place a screw eye into the foam ball before covering.

personalized baseballs

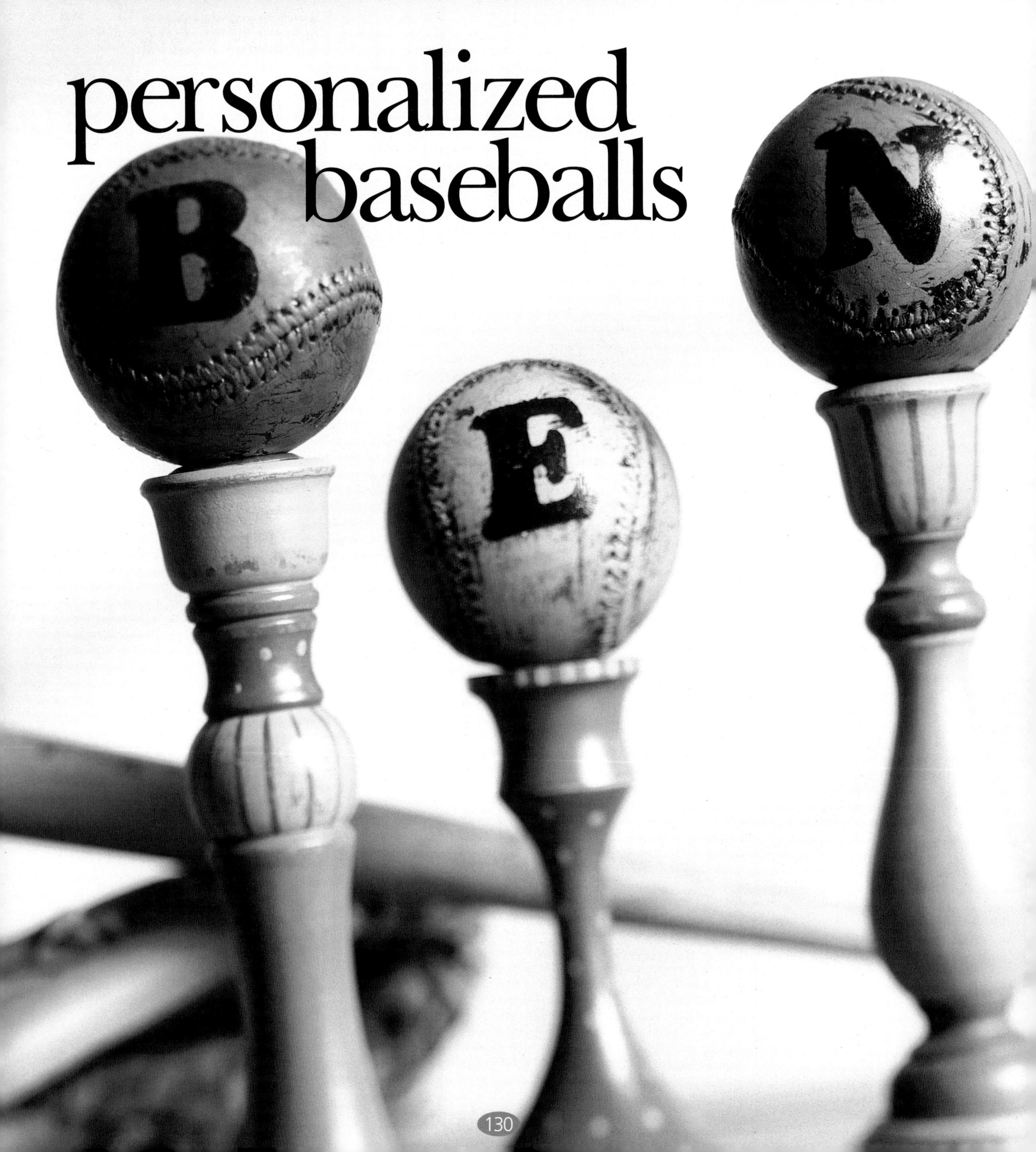

Every birthday boy or girl will be proud of these crackled baseballs or softballs that boldly display his or her name.

To make the baseballs you will need:
Baseballs or softballs, one for each letter of the desired name
Acrylic paints in black, mauve, ocher, dusty blue, or other desired colors
Medium-size flat paintbrush
Crackling medium
Vinyl adhesive letters to fit on baseballs
Small flat paintbrush
Assorted wood candleholders, one for each baseball
Fine liner paintbrush
Fine sandpaper

1 **Paint the baseballs black.** Let the paint dry. Apply a second coat if necessary. Let dry.

2 **Paint a heavy coat** of crackle medium over black paint. Let dry.

3 **Apply vinyl adhesive-back letter** to one side of the baseball, *right,* avoiding the stitched seam.

4 **Choose the color of acrylic paint** you wish to use. Using a small flat brush, paint on a medium coat of paint. Apply paint over the vinyl letter, brushing outward. Avoid brushing repeatedly over brush strokes. Allow paint to crackle as it dries. Brush paint lightly over stitching, allowing black to remain in crevices. Let dry. Gently peel away letter sticker.

5 **Paint the candleholders** in colors coordinating with the baseballs. Paint sections of the candleholders in different colors. Add dots by dipping handle end of paintbrush in paint and dotting onto surface. Paint lines using a fine liner brush. Use a small flat brush to paint checks.

6 **When all paint is dry,** lightly sand some of the edges with a fine sandpaper to create a worn look.

1 more idea...
- For a soccer keepsake, paint a soccer ball in the same manner and have teammates sign it.

also try this...
- To display the baseballs without the holders, use curtain rings to keep them from rolling.

good ideas *tiny painted vases*

Purple and lime green glass paints enhance the shapes and textures of this oil-and-vinegar set. After the simple strokes of paint are applied and dry, fill the miniature vases with water and mini bouquets.

make it in minutes

monogrammed terra-cotta pot

Keep small notes or trinkets organized with a tall flowerpot swirled gracefully with a paint pen.

To make the terra-cotta pot you will need:
- 8-inch terra-cotta pot
- White chalk
- Iridescent white paint pen
- Tracing paper
- Pencil
- Damp rag

here's how **To make this project,** use chalk to draw lines ½ and 1½ inches below the top and ½ inch from the bottom of the pot. Use paint pen to make small dots along each of the lines. Let the paint dry.

Trace the S shape from the decorative pattern, *below left,* onto tracing paper. Cut out. Use chalk to trace the S curve every 1¾ inches on the rim between the rows of dots. Paint over the chalk markings with paint pen. Let dry.

Use chalk to draw in the second curve, dot, and four small lines by each S shape. Paint over the chalk markings with paint pen. Let dry. Gently rub off any chalk markings with a damp rag. Let dry.

Use chalk to draw an initial on one side of the pot. Paint over the initial with paint pen. Let it dry. Wipe off any remaining chalk marks with a damp rag.

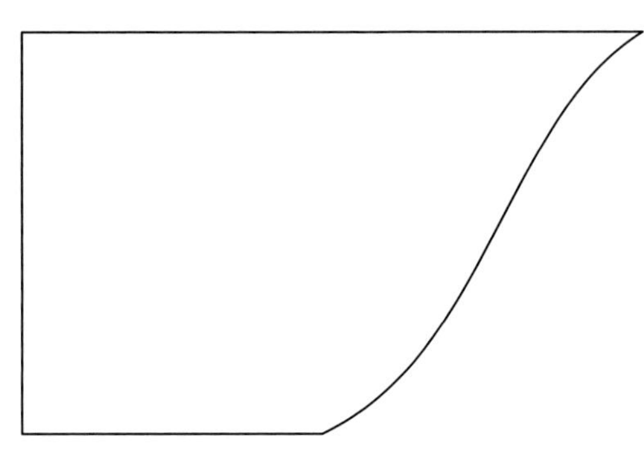

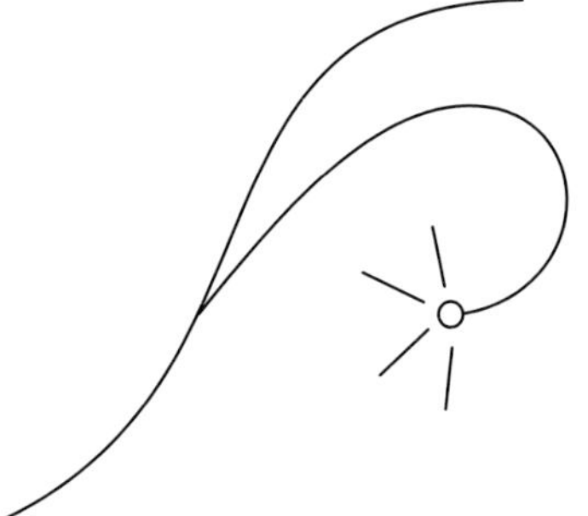

1 more idea...
- Make a pot for each member of the family to hold keys, wallets, and change.

also try this...
- For Valentine's Day, make four pots with the letters l-o-v-e and place flowers in each.

graduation gift boxes

These miniature caps have a secret compartment to hold a small gift or money for the lucky graduate.

To make a graduation cap gift box you will need:

- 4-inch-square piece of cardboard
- $2\frac{3}{4}$-inch-diameter round cardboard box
- Acrylic paints in green and black, or other desired color combination
- Flat and round paintbrushes
- Paper fastener
- Thick white crafts glue
- Ice pick
- Black tassel
- Fine liner brush

here's how **To make this project,** paint the square piece of cardboard and round cardboard box green or any desired color. Let dry. Paint a second coat if needed. Paint the lid black inside and out. Let dry. Paint the head of the paper fastener black. Let dry.

Glue the top of the lid to the center of the painted cardboard square. Using an ice pick, pierce a small hole in top center of lid, through both the glued square and the lid.

Insert the painted paper fastener through lid from the outside to inside. Loop a small black tassel around the head of the fastener. Press firmly in place and spread metal fasteners apart to hold in place.

Finish the round box by painting stripes or dots. Paint black stripes with a fine liner brush. Paint dots by dipping the handle end of a paintbrush into paint and dotting onto the surface.

1 more idea...

- For a graduation party, make several boxes in school colors and fill with candies to give to guests.

also try this...

- Write a personal message or the graduate's name and the date inside the box.

Noodle

make it in minutes

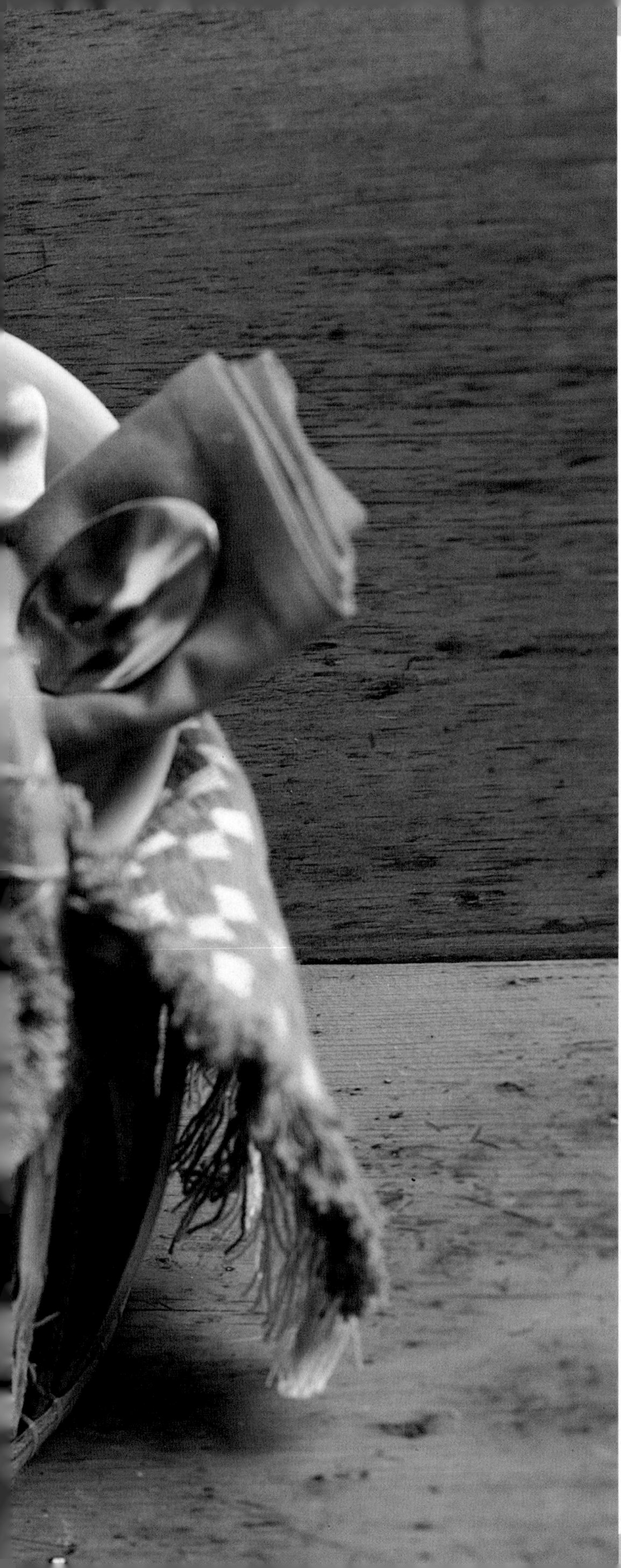

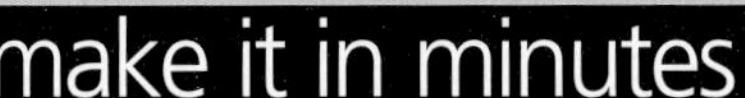

get-well basket

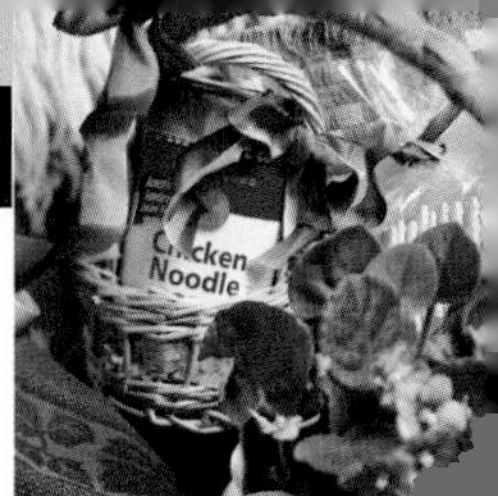

To make the basket you will need:

Cloth place mat or large napkin
Large basket
Small basket to hold a soup can
Ribbon
Canned soup, flowers, and other get-well items

Bring a basket of sunshine to someone who's feeling a bit under the weather.

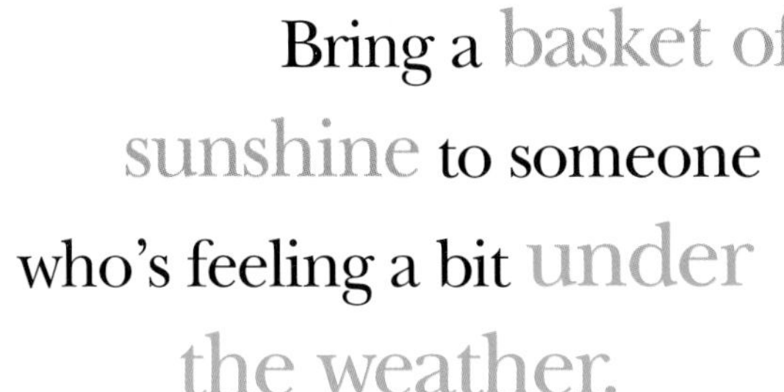

here's how **To make this project,** line the large basket with a cloth place mat or napkin. Place a can of soup in the smaller basket and tie the handles of the two baskets together using a generous length of ribbon.

Arrange the remaining items in the basket. Add an additional ribbon bow or two if desired.

1 more idea...

- To make a basket for a child, include coloring books, crayons, a puppet, playing cards, and a handheld electronic game.

also try this...

- For a "moving" basket, include an address book, maps, packing tape, and a gift certificate for a restaurant near the owners' new home.

spring blooms tray

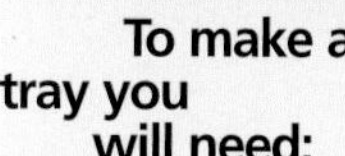

Celebrate spring's magic by preserving blooms to embellish a painted tray.

To make a tray you will need:
Flowers for drying, such as delphinium, yellow daisies, four-o'clocks, ferns, and leaves
Heavy book
Tin tray
White spray primer
Small natural sponge
Water
Disposable foam plate
Acrylic paints in rosy pink, golden ocher, and creamy ivory
Paintbrush
Decoupage medium

1 **Prepare flowers ahead of time.** Press flowers such as yellow daisies, four-o'clocks, and delphinium in a heavy book overnight. Press ferns and various leaves in the same manner.

2 **Wash and dry the tray.** Prime the front with white spray primer. Let it dry.

3 **To sponge-paint the tray,** use a small natural sponge, soak it with water, and squeeze out excess. Place a small amount of rosy pink, golden ocher, and creamy ivory on plate. Using the rosy pink color, begin sponging on the outer edge and sponge inward. Next, sponge the ocher color, blending the colors together. Do not allow the paint to dry between colors. Blend the colors in toward the center, adding cream last. The tray will be pinker on the outer edges and lighter toward the center. Let the paint dry.

4 **Decide how to arrange** the flowers on the tray. Apply a coat of decoupage medium to the tray, beginning in the center and working outward. Lay flowers down into wet decoupage medium. Arrange fern pieces and leaves directing outward. Arrange leaves in a border around the rim of tray. Let decoupage medium dry.

5 **Apply at least two or three** more coats of decoupage medium over tray front, allowing to dry between coats.

1 more idea...

- Make one-of-a-kind frames and picture mats by decoupaging pressed items on the fronts.

also try this...

- For a Christmas tray, clip out words and holiday motifs from old Christmas cards.

pearlized easter eggs

Easter gatherings are the perfect time to display this elegant egg centerpiece.

To make these eggs you will need:
Eggs, real or plaster
Tiny nail, bowl
Pearlized acrylic paints in yellow, pink, white, blue, green, and lavender
Disposable foam plate
Sponge and water
Glass bowl
White sand
Pearls and shells

1 **Pierce tiny holes** on opposite ends of an egg if using real eggs. Poke a hole in the egg yolk. Blow the inside of egg into a bowl. Discard or use the inside.

2 **Choose color combinations** for your eggs. These pearlized colors were used in combinations of three colors: yellow, white, and pink; yellow, white, and green; pink, white, and lavender; lavender, white, and blue; and blue, white, and green.

3 **Place the three colors of paint** on a foam plate. Use small amounts, about the size of a quarter. Soak a sponge in water and squeeze out the excess. Begin sponging on one color on one end, as *above*, rinse out sponge, and apply the other color.

4 **Add and sponge in white** where you want colors to lighten, as at *left*. Sponge and blend colors together until the desired look is achieved.

5 **Display the eggs** in a glass bowl with white sand, shells, and pearls.

1 more idea...

- Display the soft-toned eggs in a grouping, placed in different styles of egg holders.

also try this...

- Use this same technique to give ordinary Christmas balls an artful touch.

nifty needle books

A perfect little gift for Mother's Day, these sweet needle holders are made from scraps of felt, embroidery floss, and mismatched buttons.

To make a needle book you will need:
- Scraps of felt
- Pinking shears
- Paper punch
- 2 eyelets and eyelet tool
- Cotton embroidery floss
- Needle
- Assortment of buttons
- Tracing paper
- Pencil

here's how **To make this project,** use a pinking shears to cut the outside felt piece to 6×3¾ inches. Cut a 5×3-inch piece of contrasting felt for the inside.

With the smaller piece centered on the larger one, use a paper punch to make a hole 1 inch from the top center and another 1 inch from the bottom center. From the outside, place an eyelet through each hole, going through both layers of felt. Use an eyelet tool to secure each eyelet.

Using the photograph for ideas, decide on the cover design. Use embroidery floss to sew on buttons. If you wish to make the flower and leaf design, trace the leaf pattern, *left*. Use the pattern to cut one leaf from green felt. Sew to cover using running stitches.

To embroider a name or initial, trace and transfer the desired letters from *pages 146–147*. Use a chain stitch to make initials and a couching stitch to sew a tiny name (see diagrams, *below*).

Cut an 8x¼-inch piece of felt. Thread it through both eyelets and knot on the outside of the cover. Trim the ends.

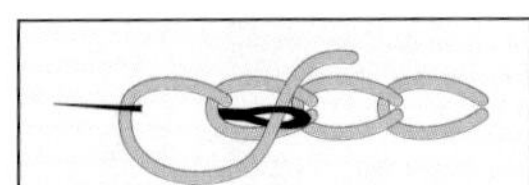

Chain Stitch

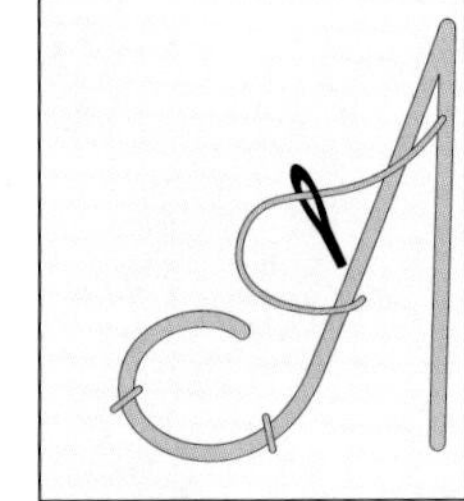

Couching

1 more idea...
- Use paper instead of felt to make small drawing books for children.

also try this...
- Personalize the needle book covers by adding meaningful charms.

Mom
R

nifty needle books (continued)

You'll need to enlarge this pattern 118%

You'll need to enlarge this pattern 118%

rainbow cup and trivet

A great housewarming gift, these kitchen necessities come alive with strokes of vibrant paint.

To make the cup and trivet you will need:
Soup mug
White tile
Glass paints in purple, bright pink, green, orange, blue, and yellow
Paintbrush
Tracing paper
Pencil
Lightweight cardboard
Crafts knife
Sponge
Four 1-inch-diameter wood knobs
Epoxy

1 more idea...

- Paint a matching set of soup mugs for a housewarming gift.

also try this...

- As long as food or drink does not directly touch the paint, use these techniques to paint trays, plates, and silverware handles.

here's how **To make this project,** wash and dry the soup mug and the tile. Avoid touching the areas to be painted.

Using a small flat paintbrush, paint stripes around the top portion of the soup mug as shown, *left*. Alternate the paint colors and make the strokes uneven. Let dry.

Trace the star pattern, *below*, onto tracing paper. Transfer to lightweight cardboard and carefully cut out star shape with a crafts knife to make a stencil.

Place stencil on the top of the tile. Use a dampened sponge dipped in yellow paint and dab over star stencil. Stencil as many yellow stars on the tile top as desired. Let dry.

Sponge around the stars using blue paint. Let dry.

Add stripes to the edge of the tile in the same manner as on the mug. Let dry.

Paint the wood knobs yellow. Let dry. Add orange dots by dipping the handle end of the paintbrush into paint and dotting onto the surface. Let dry. Glue a knob to each corner of the tile back. Let dry.

cute-as-a-button candles

Zigzags of wire surround any size of pillar candle, while buttons of all kinds add interest to the weathered-looking wire.

To make a candle you will need:

- Drill
- Cup hook
- Wire
- Pillar candle
- Wire cutters
- Buttons
- Hot-glue gun and hot-glue sticks

here's how **To make this project,** place a cup hook in a drill and tighten. Bend an 80-inch length of wire in half. Place the loop over the cup hook. Secure the wire ends in a vise. Pulling firmly on the drill, turn it on to twist the wire. Remove from cup hook.

Bend the wire back and forth the height of the candle. When the bent wire will wrap around the candle, cut the wire. Secure the ends together.

Glue buttons onto wire as desired. Let dry. Slip the candle inside the ring.

1 more idea...

- Instead of buttons, use old or secondhand earrings as embellishments.

also try this...

- Use this same technique to trim vases, winding wire around the shape.

good ideas *picket fence valance*

Purchased fencing takes its place indoors as a creative window topper. Secure the fence section to a window frame, then embellish it with artificial vines and berries to bring the outdoors in. For a splash of color, add a fabric valance below.

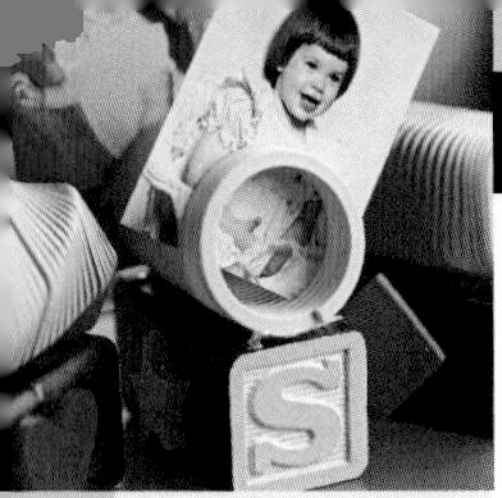

playful picture holders

Creatively display children's pictures by tucking them into a toy perched on a wood block.

To make the holder you will need:
- Wood blocks
- Thick white crafts glue
- Acrylic paint in black and other desired colors
- Paintbrush
- Wood stars, hearts, squares, or other desired shapes
- Plastic ringed toy
- Clear gloss sealer spray
- Hot-glue gun and hot-glue sticks

here's how **To make this project,** glue two blocks together. If using letter blocks, place letter side on each end. Paint the sides with black paint.

Paint wood shapes in colors complementary to the plastic ringed toy. Let the paint dry. Glue the shapes to the sides of the blocks. Let dry. Spray with a coat of sealer. Let dry.

Apply a line of hot glue across the top of each end of the blocks. Press each end of the plastic ringed toy into the glue. Let dry.

1 more idea...
- Use a metallic ringed toy and metallic paints to make a holder for an office desk.

also try this...
- To use the photo holder in a child's room, trim the blocks with miniature toys.

punch-it-out note cards

Send a personal May Day note on a cheery card you make using a variety of paper punches and scraps of colorful papers.

To make a note card you will need:

- Scissors
- Paper scraps
- Decorative-edge scissors
- Round, heart-shape, or other desired paper punches
- Thick white crafts glue
- Toothpick
- Fine-point permanent marking pen in desired color

here's how **To make this project,** cut the background paper approximately 3¾x5¼ inches. Fold the paper piece in half.

Use decorative-edge scissors to cut a rectangle smaller than the card front. Use desired paper punch to make designs on paper using the photo, *above*, for ideas.

To make leaves, cut small leaf shapes from green paper. To give the leaves dimension, fold them in half from point to point.

Glue the rectangle in the center of the card front. Add punched shapes and leaves, using a toothpick to apply glue to the tiny pieces. Write desired message on the front and inside of the card.

1 more idea...

- To use these cards as gift tags, make one-sided and add a hole punch to attach a cord or ribbon.

also try this...

- Use cookie cutters as patterns to cut tags into shapes, such as hearts and flowers.

beautiful bookmarks

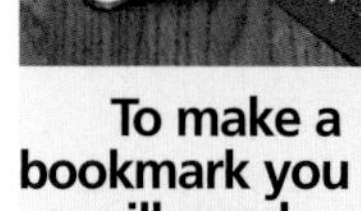

From confirmations to first communions, these lovely bookmarks send a meaningful message, foiled in gold.

To make a bookmark you will need:

- Suede or imitation cloth suede scraps in any color
- Decorative-edge scissors, pinking shears, or straight scissors
- Pencil
- Adhesive, such as Plaid Foil Bond
- Foil, such as Plaid Press & Peel Foil
- Sealer, such as Liquid Beads Sealer for Press & Peel Foil
- Fine liner paintbrush
- Eyelet and eyelet tool
- Gold floss or thread
- Beads to coordinate with suede

1 **Cut the suede** to measure 7×2¼ inches. You can cut with decorative-edge scissors, pinking shears, or straight scissors. Round the corners, if desired.

2 **Decide what design** or words to write on the bookmark. Practice on paper first. Draw the design on the bookmark using pencil. If using a light-colored suede, use a standard lead pencil. On dark suede, use a light-color pencil.

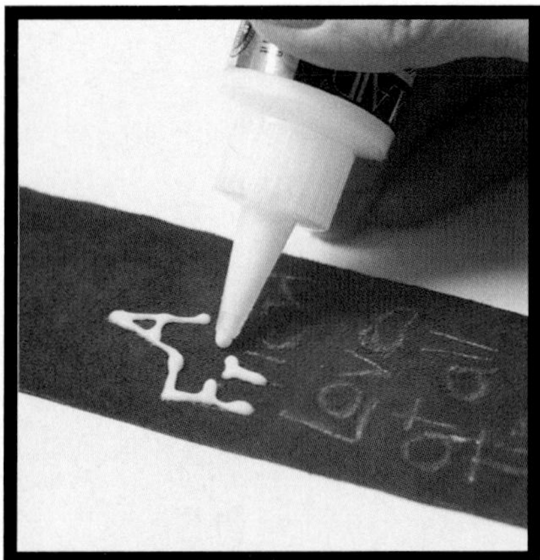

3 **Draw over pencil lines** with adhesive. This adhesive will look white. When it turns clear and tacky it is ready to have the gold foil applied. The adhesive should be tacky and firm, unable to be smeared.

4 **Lay foil over the adhesive,** placing the dull side against adhesive. Rub firmly over top of foil sheet with fingers until the gold foil is released onto the adhesive. Repeat this process until finished. Apply sealer over foil, using a fine liner brush.

5 **Using a pencil,** make a mark for the eyelet, ¾ inch from the top. Clip a small X over the mark with scissors.

6 **Insert the eyelet** into the hole and secure using the tool. Cut a length of gold decorative floss approximately 10 inches long. Tie a bead on one end, leaving a 2-inch tail of thread. String beads on thread to cover approximately 6 inches. Pull beaded string through eyelet and tie on the last bead. Tie the tails together, keeping beads taut. Trim tails even.

1 more idea...

- For a child's birthday, draw the number that corresponds to the birthday.

also try this...

- To create a quick finishing touch, tie a purchased tassel through the eyelet.

golden eggs

Striking designs and vivid colors team up to create eye-catching Easter eggs.

To make the eggs you will need:

Eggs
Nail
Bowl
Long wooden skewer
Gold spray paint
Stickers in desired shapes
Scissors
Masking tape
Model car metallic spray paints in pink, purple, teal, or other desired colors

here's how **To make this project,** pierce a small hole on each end of egg with a tiny nail. Pierce the yolk. Blow out the insides into a bowl. Discard or use the inside.

Wash and dry the egg, making sure the inside is empty. Gently insert a long wooden skewer into one end of the egg to hold while painting. Spray the egg with 2 or 3 light coats of gold spray paint, allowing the paint to dry between coats.

Apply stickers or squares of masking tape to the egg as desired to create the gold designs. Gently push down the edges. Lightly spray the egg with a desired color of spray paint. Spray 2 or 3 very light coats if needed. Let dry. Remove stickers and carefully remove from skewer.

1 more idea...

- Reverse the painting process, using gold for the top coat.

also try this...

- Use this same technique on round glass Christmas ornaments.

easter surprise pens

The Easter bunny will create lots of smiles when he perches these adorable pens in Easter baskets.

To make a pen you will need:
Pencil
Tracing paper
Scissors
Craft foam in pink, pale pink, yellow, white, purple, blue, and green
Smooth round ink pens
Hot-glue gun and hot-glue sticks
Chenille stems
Paper punch
Black permanent fine-line marking pen

1 **Trace the desired pattern**, *pages 160–161,* onto tracing paper. Cut out the shapes and trace onto the coordinating color of foam. Cut out the foam pieces.

2 **Cut a foam strip** ½×8 inches. If desired, alternate ¼- and ½-inch-wide strips of different colors. Secure one colored strip on one end of the pen with hot glue, *above*. If desired, glue a coordinating strip alongside the first strip. Continue to wind and glue the strips on the pen until covered. Trim both ends even. If desired, add a coordinating strip of foam at the end, as on the flower pen.

3 **For all pens,** prepare the three small foam pieces that fit at the end of the pen. Layer a square, small circle, and square for the bunny, the 3 small circles for the flower, or a notched circle, small plain circle, and remaining notched circle for the chick. Pierce 2 small holes with the tip of sharp scissors into the foam through all layers, as if they had buttonholes.

4 **Insert the chenille stem** through one hole, pushing through all 3 layers. Pull stem halfway through. Push the end of chenille stem back through the other hole. Glue to pen top.

5 **For the flower,** glue the leaf to one stem. Glue the other stem to the center of large pink flower. Layer and glue the orange flower shape, the small pink flower shape, and yellow center to cover the chenille stem. Punch out small purple dots with a paper punch and glue onto yellow center.

6 **To make the bunny,** sandwich the chenille stems between the front and back pieces of the bow tie, as *above*. Glue on the remaining head pieces and dots on the bow tie. Draw the mouth.

7 **To make the chick,** glue small head to body. Glue on orange beak. Punch out a purple eye with a paper punch and glue onto the head. Glue the chick onto one purple egg shell. Glue the two chenille stems onto the front of chick and egg. Glue on the other egg shell to cover stems, gluing around the edges.

1 more idea...

- Make the foam toppers and add a pin back for a fun Easter pin.

also try this...

- Glue the foam toppers to toothpicks for cupcake or cake decorations.

easter surprise pens (continued)

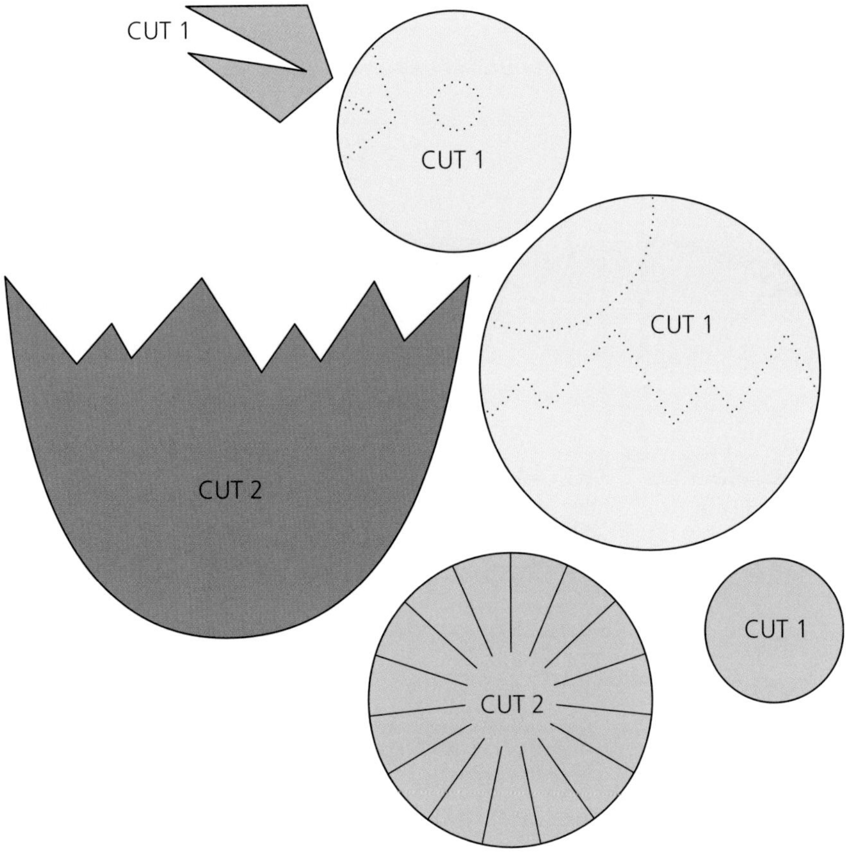

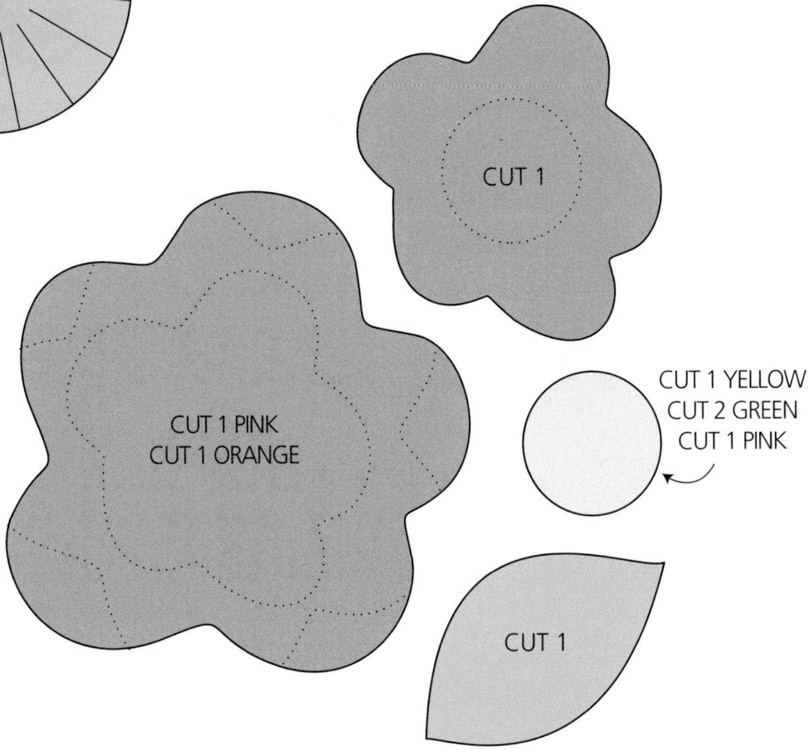

CUT 1

CUT 1

CUT 1

CUT 2

CUT 2

CUT 1

PLACEMENT DIAGRAM

CUT 1

PLACEMENT DIAGRAM

CUT 1 PINK
CUT 1 ORANGE

CUT 1 YELLOW
CUT 2 GREEN
CUT 1 PINK

CUT 1

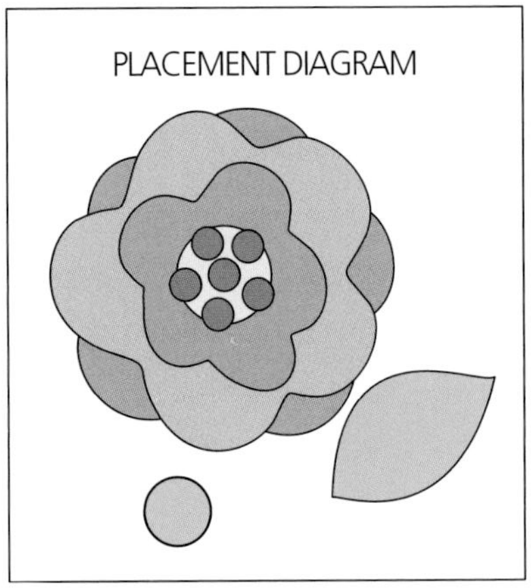

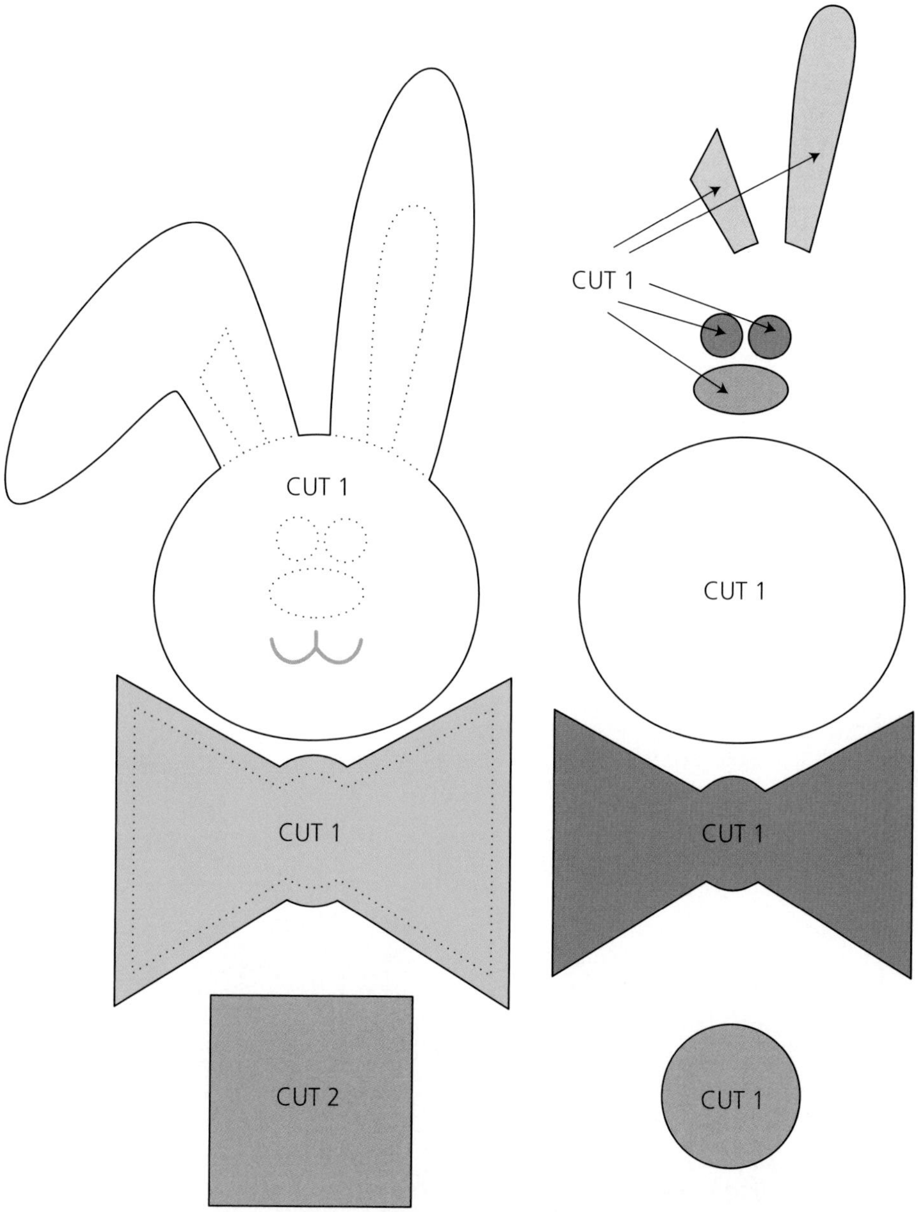

CUT 1

CUT 1

CUT 1

CUT 1

CUT 1

CUT 2

CUT 1

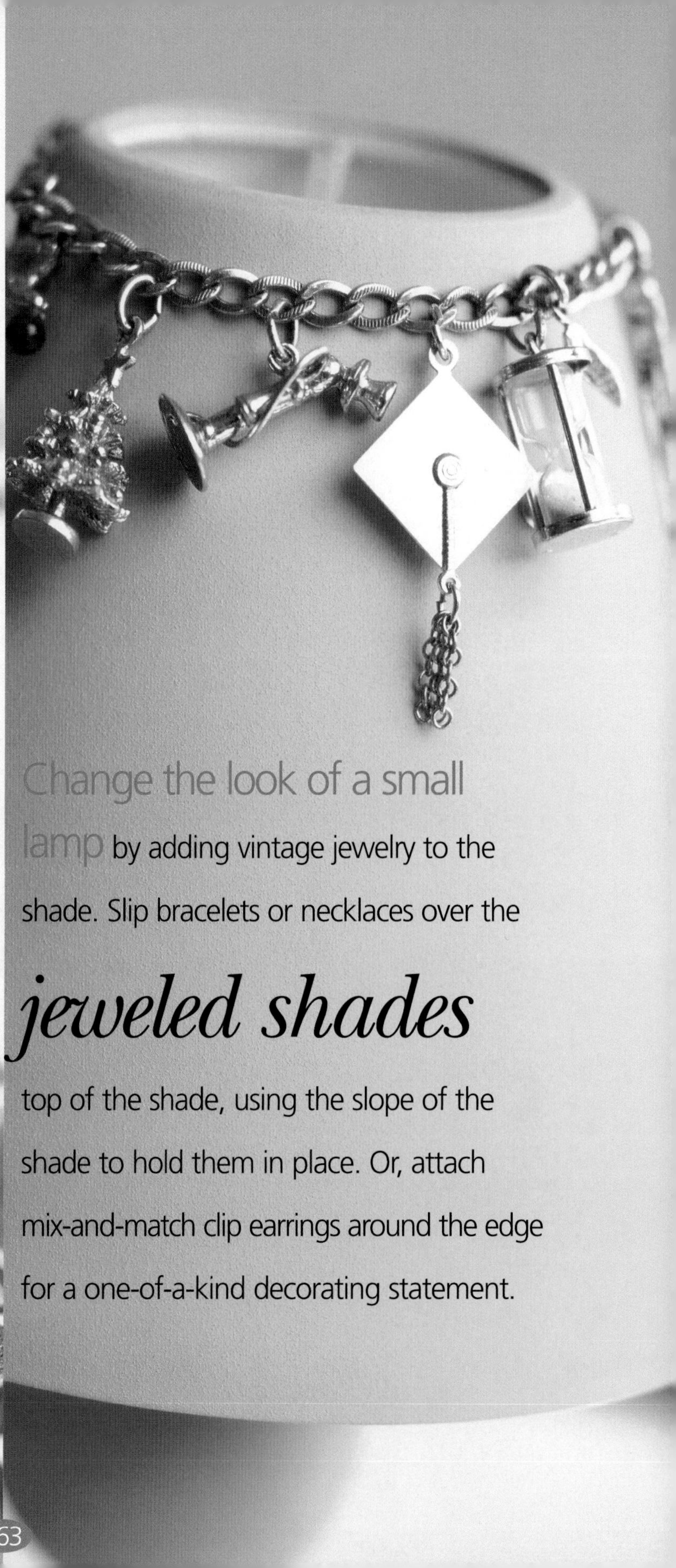

good ideas *jeweled shades*

Change the look of a small lamp by adding vintage jewelry to the shade. Slip bracelets or necklaces over the top of the shade, using the slope of the shade to hold them in place. Or, attach mix-and-match clip earrings around the edge for a one-of-a-kind decorating statement.

nighty-night light

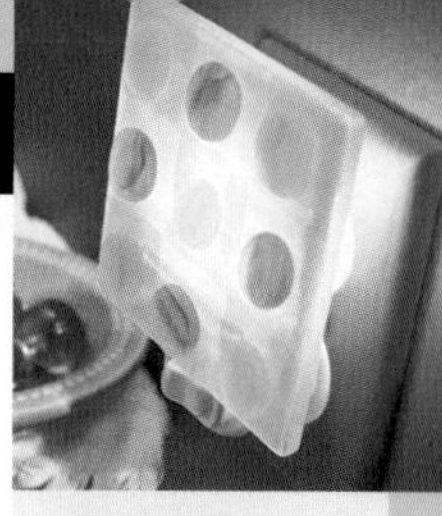

Flat glass marbles, available in a rainbow of colors, let the light shine through on this lovely night-light.

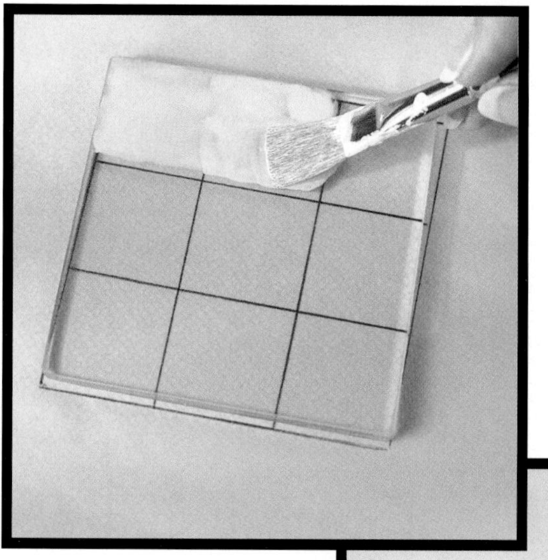

1 Trace around the glass square onto tracing paper. Use a ruler to divide evenly into nine squares as shown, *left.* Place the pattern under the glass and paint the squares. You can paint the white first, if desired. Let it dry. Use the grid to paint the yellow. Let dry. If instructed by the paint manufacturer, bake the painted glass piece in the oven.

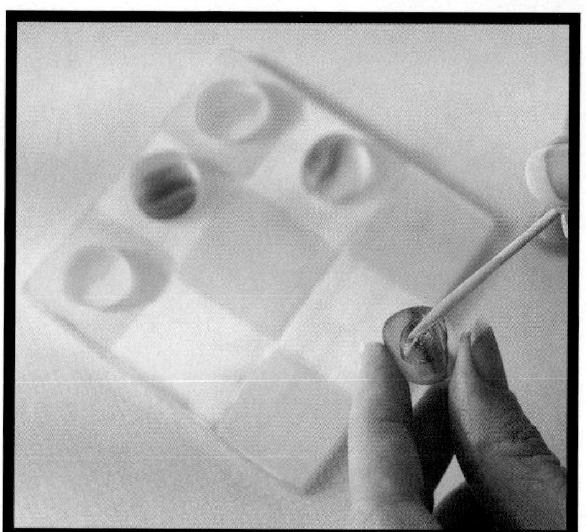

2 After the glass piece has cooled, mix a small amount of epoxy. Using a toothpick, apply a small dab to the back of a marble and place in the center of a painted square. Continue adding marbles in this manner until all of the squares are filled. Let the epoxy dry.

3 Attach the glass piece to the night-light fixture using epoxy. Allow the epoxy to set up for 24 hours before using.

To make a night-light you will need:

3¼-inch-square piece of 3/16-inch-thick glass with sanded edges
Tracing paper
Pencil
Ruler
Glass or ceramic paints in white and yellow
Paintbrush
Clear epoxy glue
Toothpick
Flat marbles in frosted blue and green (available in crafts and home decor stores)
Night-light fixture (available in hardware stores)

1 more idea...

- For a child's room, use a variety of colored marbles and paint smiley faces on each using glass paint.

also try this...

- To create a flower design, put one marble in the center and use smaller marbles around it to form petals.

woven bag

A perfect size to keep little things organized in your purse, this jewel-tone bag is made by weaving bits and pieces of ribbon.

To make the bag you will need:
Scissors
¼ yard of lightweight fusible interfacing
Pins
Cardboard
Approximately 9 yards of desired ribbon, ¼ to 1½ inches wide
Fusible hemming tape
Iron
7×17-inch piece of lining fabric
Thread to match ribbons
Snap
Decorative button

1 **Cut a 7×17-inch piece** of interfacing. Pin the interfacing, fusible side up, to the cardboard.

2 **Cut enough 17-inch-long ribbons** to cover the interfacing. Pin the ribbons side by side atop the interfacing as shown.

3 **Cut several ribbons** to a length of 7 inches. Pin fusible hem tape to the ribbon backs.

4 **Begin weaving short ribbons** with those pinned to the cardboard. Pin the ribbon ends as the weaving is completed.

5 **Using an iron,** fuse the ribbons to the interfacing, removing the pins as you go. Trim the edges even if necessary.

6 **Place the lining fabric** atop the woven ribbon piece, right sides facing. Stitch together using a ¼-inch seam allowance and leaving one short end open. Trim the seams and turn.

7 **Measure 6½ inches** from the stitched short end. Fold the woven piece at this point with the right sides facing. Hand-stitch both side seams. Turn right side out.

8 **To make the flap point,** measure 2½ inches from the open end on each side. Fold the corners together and stitch from marked sides to the center of the flap. Turn right side out.

9 **Sew on a snap closure** where the flap point meets the bag. Sew a decorative button to the point of the flap.

1 more idea...

- For an extra-special gift, use the bag as the wrap for a piece of jewelry.

also try this...

- Decorate the point of the bag flap with a lapel pin.

good ideas *delightful doilies*

Add a splash of color to purchased white or ivory doilies. Place imitation cloth suede, felt, or paper under the doily and trim the background fabric just beyond the doily edge. Glue in place or use tiny stitches to hold the layers together.

make it in minutes

springtime vase

To make the vase you will need:
White bud vase
Glass paints in black, bright pink, purple, and yellow
Paintbrush

Jazzy stripes and dots turn a plain white vase into a striking container for spring flowers.

here's how **To make this project,** paint the rings of the vase using different colors. Let the paint dry between coats. To paint stripes, paint vertical strokes, leaving white between each.

To add small dots at the base, dip the handle end of a paintbrush into paint and dot onto the surface.

For the squares, make short strokes with a flat paintbrush. Let the paint dry. Bake in the oven if directed by the paint manufacturer.

1 more idea...

- For special get-togethers, paint a set of teacups or coffee or soup mugs using these techniques.

also try this...

- If starting with a clear glass vase, paint it white and let it dry before adding the stripes and dots of color.

fresh floating candles

Fresh from the garden—or the grocer's shelves—fruits and flowers add a refreshing touch to floating candles.

To make a floating candle you will need:

Glass container or vase
Fresh fruit or flowers
Water
Floating candle

here's how **To make this project,** fill the glass container approximately halfway with desired fruit or fresh flower heads. If using lemons or limes, slice them before placing into the container.

Carefully fill the container with water, leaving about 2 inches at the top. Place a floating candle on top of the water.

1 more idea...

- For a child's birthday party, fill glass container with marbles or small plastic toys.

also try this...

- For extra sparkle, sprinkle the water with glitter before adding the candle.

more ideas *for* spring

- Use fabric paints to add strokes of color to a plain umbrella.
- Check your supply of paintbrushes; replace those that are badly worn.
- Teach a child how to plant flower seeds, and keep a garden journal to track their progress.
- Decoupage emptied seed packets on the outside of a wood planter to hold gardening tools.
- Encourage the kids to help wash all the vehicles and bikes.
- Search flea markets for unmatched wood candlesticks, and paint them with bright acrylic paints to make a grouping.

- Plan a family crafting night and stock up on all necessary crafts supplies.

- Give an old dresser or cabinet a new look by freshening with a coat of paint and decoupaging on the details.

- To hardboil eggs without cracking, place eggs in a pan of cold water before turning on the burner.

- Use glass paints to add simple designs to jars, bottles, and vases to hold fresh or artificial bouquets.

- Nestle a votive candle in a bowl of jelly beans for Easter.

- Decorate a plain or check tablecloth with paint pens for both outdoor and indoor picnics.

Summer afternoon–summer afternoon;
to me those have always been the two most
beautiful words in the English language.

— HENRY JAMES

summer

As the warmth of summer's sun envelopes the days, take the time to make these creative projects for yourself and those you love. You may even learn a new technique or two that you can share with a friend on a rainy day.

Personalize a clock by framing the face with gold metal charms. Readily available in crafts stores, the charms can be glued on using an all-purpose adhesive. Remove any hanging loops on the charms by bending with pliers.

good ideas *charming clocks*

sand candles

Twisted wire makes strong hangers for these candles nestled in colored sand.

To make a candle hanger you will need:

- Cup hook
- Hand drill
- 24-gauge steel or copper wire
- Wire cutters
- C-clamp
- Needle-nose pliers
- Beads and rhinestones
- Small jar
- Jewelry glue
- Colored sand
- Votive candle

1 **Insert the cup hook** into the drill and tighten.

2 **Make two sets of banding wires** to go around the neck of the jar by cutting two 12-inch pieces of wire for each set. Holding two of the pieces together, make a loop in the wires 3 inches from the ends. Measure 3 inches up from the opposite end. Clamp the end to a work surface with a C-clamp. Slip the looped end of the wires over the cup hook in the drill. Use the drill to twist the two wires together. Remove the wire from cup hook and clamp. Untwist the ends of loop, using pliers to straighten out the ends.

3 **For the hanging wire,** cut a 36-inch length of wire and fold in half. Clamp loose ends to the table top, slip folded end over the cup hook in drill, and twist the wire together. Remove from cup hook and clamp. Determine the length of the hanger, and fold wire in half. A bead can be added if desired. Bend loose ends up to make both sides of the hanger even. Twist ends around the wire several times, leaving a small loop at the bend. Cut off excess wire.

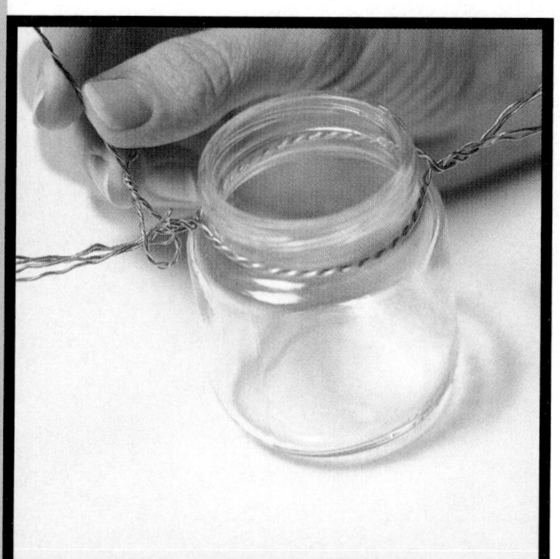

4 **Wrap one banding wire** around half of the jar top and the second banding wire around the other half. Slip loose ends of both sets of banding wires through the loop on one side of the hanging wire. Twist the end of the wire around the hanging wire, just above the loop. Do not cut off the excess wire. Repeat the process for the other side of the hanging wire, making sure the banding wire is tightly secured around the neck of the jar.

5 **Slip bead onto the excess lengths** of the banding wire, twisting the wires around the bead. Use the needle-nose pliers to twist some of the wire into a spiral.

6 **Glue rhinestones** to the jar sides. Let the glue dry. Fill halfway with sand and place a votive candle in the center.

1 more idea...

- For May Day, fill the jars with shredded colored paper and wrapped candies or straw flowers.

also try this...

- Omit the wire hangers to make walkway luminarias for any season.

oh-so-cute baby shoes

Imagine how precious your little angel will look wearing these whimsically painted shoes.

To make the shoes you will need:
White baby shoes
Glossy acrylic paints in lime green, teal green, lavender, black, white, turquoise, yellow, and pink
Small flat paintbrushes
Fine liner brush

here's how **To make this project,** begin with a clean white pair of baby shoes. Remove shoelaces before painting.

To paint the striped decorative edge around bottom, paint a solid area first in lime green. Let the paint dry. Add stripes over top using teal green and a small flat paintbrush. Let the paint dry. Add lavender stripes over teal green using a narrower fine paintbrush. Let dry.

Paint the shoe top/tongue solid black. Let dry. Add white dots by dipping the handle end of paintbrush into paint and dotting on the surface.

Paint the side panels turquoise. Let dry. Paint a yellow sun on the turquoise. Paint a circle first, then make short strokes around circle with a fine paintbrush.

Paint pink and yellow stripes around top, and trim with pink and yellow checks around stitched areas. Let dry. Lace with colored laces.

1 more idea...

- Use a permanent marker to write nursery rhymes sayings around the shoes, using the seams as guides.

also try this...

- For your little sports fan, write, "Go, Team!" in the appropriate team colors on the shoes.

good ideas *cheer-filled cups*

For a quick yet elegant gift for a coffee lover, fill a pretty cup with coffee beans. Wrap the cup and saucer with cellophane and tie at the top with a ribbon bow.

pom-pom pillow

With a belt buckle holding them in place, these colorful ribbon pom-poms dress up any ordinary purchased pillow.

To make a pillow you will need:

Purchased pillow
Assorted ribbons
Large belt buckle
Felt
Beads
Scissors

1 **Wrap desired ribbon** around the pillow. Cross the ribbons on the back side and bring back around to the front. Tie the ribbon ends onto the buckle. Keep the buckle positioned in the middle.

2 **Add loops and bows** of various widths and colors of ribbons, attaching them all to the buckle. Strips cut from felt with pinking shears, approximately 2×8 inches, may also be used.

3 **String beads onto a thin ribbon** and tie to the buckle. To make a beaded bow, string enough beads onto a ribbon to make a piece 13 inches long. Leave 2 inches without beads. Slide beads apart to create an empty bead space in the middle. Loop each end around to make a bow, crossing the tails in the center. Take another ribbon about 5 inches long and tie it tightly around the folded bow in the center. Tie the beaded bow to the center of the buckle.

4 **To neatly trim ribbon ends,** fold the ribbon in half lengthwise. Starting at the fold, make a slanted cut toward the outer edges of the ribbon.

1 more idea...

- Make seasonal pillow wraps by choosing different color schemes for each season.

also try this...

- This project is fun for kids when using school colors.

good ideas *jelly bean tins*

Great for party favors or last-minute gifts, these tiny tins double as candy holders for extra-sweet treats. Fill the miniature gelatin molds with colorful jelly beans, wrap in cellophane, and tie with a ribbon bow.

make it in minutes

stamped desk accessories

Postage stamps from countries around the globe adorn these desk accessories for dear ol' dad.

To make the stamp ball and pencil holder you will need:

- Cancelled or new postage stamps, with any backings removed
- 5-inch-diameter foam ball, such as Styrofoam
- Glossy decoupage medium
- Paintbrush
- Armature wire
- Wire cutters
- Lead-free solder
- Silver-colored pencil holder
- Scissors

here's how **To make this project,** begin by decoupaging stamps on the foam ball. Cover a small area of the foam ball with decoupage medium. Place and overlap stamps onto this area, painting over the top with more decoupage medium. Continue adding stamps in this manner until the entire ball is covered.

To make the stand, cut three 16-inch lengths from armature wire. Bend the ends into coils as shown, *above*. If necessary, adjust the coils so all three wires are the same length. Holding the armature wires with the coils outward, wrap the straight sections with lead-free solder to secure. Adjust the wire legs of the stand so it stands straight.

For the pencil holder, decoupage a row of stamps around the center of the holder. Trim stamps, if needed, to maintain a straight edge. If desired, wrap solder or armature wire around the holder, to add a finished edge to the stamped area. Curl the ends of the wire as desired.

1 more idea...

- For a kids' project, use a rubber ball and stickers instead.

also try this...

- To make a container for new postage stamps, decoupage a small container with stamps, adding addresses torn from handwritten envelopes.

silver-trimmed pots

Give ordinary terra-cotta pots a quick removable facelift by adding metal trims to the rims.

To make the pots you will need:
- Tape measure
- Terra-cotta flower pots
- Straight-edge and decorative-edge scissors
- Crafting aluminum (available at hobby and crafts stores)
- Paper punch
- Eyelets and eyelet tool
- Crafting wire
- Key chain
- Permanent black marking pen

here's how **To make the pot** with the solid rim band, measure around the rim of the pot. Cut a piece of aluminum 2 inches wide and 1 inch longer than the measurement. Be careful when handling the aluminum as the edges can be sharp.

Use a paper punch to make a hole every 2 inches, ½ inch from the bottom edge. Punch out holes every 2 inches along the top edge, between those on the bottom. Place an eyelet in each hole and secure with the eyelet tool.

Wrap the metal band around the pot rim and use wire to lace the holes together where the ends overlap.

To make the multiband rimmed pot and tag, cut 5-inch-long pieces from metal, ½ to 1½ inches wide. Cut one end to a point. Punch a hole and add an eyelet to each point. Fold the metal strips in half. Place over the lip of the rim and press to form to the shape of the rim.

To make a tag, cut a rectangular piece from aluminum. Punch a hole and add an eyelet to one corner. Thread a key chain through hole. Write identifying word on tag using a permanent black marking pen.

1 more idea...
- Make garden stakes in the same manner as the tag by adding a second eyelet below the first and threading the tag onto a metal rod.

also try this...
- Use colored eyelets to add a splash of color to the pot trims.

paisley rugs

Show off your style on area rugs with pretty paisley designs painted in your favorite colors.

To make a rug you will need:
Tracing paper
Pencil
Medium-weight cardboard
Area rug with subtle design
Acrylic paints in desired colors
Disposable foam plate
Textile medium
Paintbrushes
Pencil with round-tip eraser

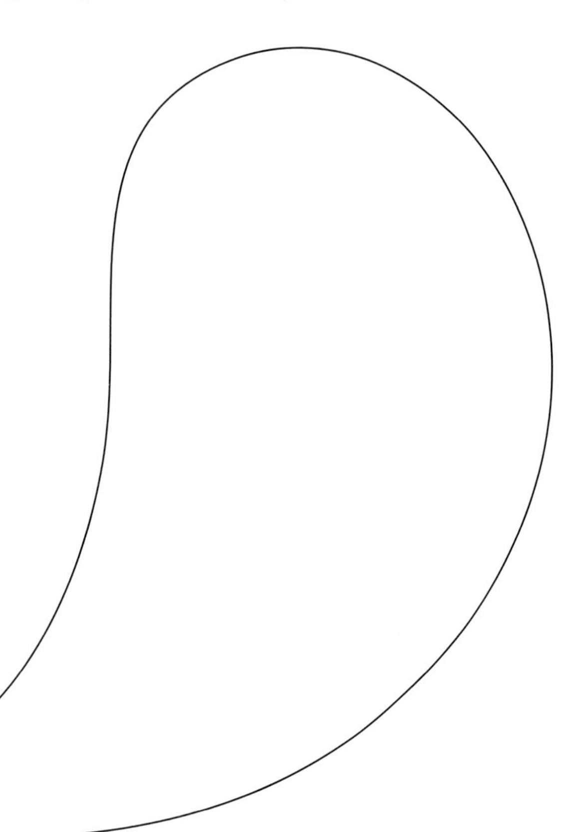

here's how **To make this project,** trace the pattern, *left.* Transfer to cardboard and cut out.

Decide how to paint the rug. Place the designs randomly over the entire rug or only around the edges. Lay the cardboard pattern on the rug and trace around it wherever you want to paint a paisley design.

Place a small amount of the paint color to be used for the paisley background on a foam plate. Mix the paint with textile medium according to the manufacturer's directions. Paint in the paisley shapes. Let the paint dry.

Use accent colors of paint to add details to the paisley shapes as well as small shapes between the paisleys, such as triangles. To add small dots, dip the eraser end of a pencil into paint and dot onto the surface. Let the paint dry.

1 more idea...

- For seasonal changes, paint the back of the rug in another color scheme.

also try this...

- Paint designs from coloring books to match your decor, such as flowers, butterflies, and ladybugs.

LAND OF
FRUITS

marbleized shades

With a couple of easy steps you can add swirls of color to purchased lampshades—giving them an elegant marbleized look.

To make a lampshade you will need:
Metal pan
Liquid starch
Acrylic paints in desired colors
Skewer
Small lampshade
Waxed paper

1 **Pour liquid starch** into the metal pan, filling about 1 inch. Drip desired colors of paint into starch. If the paint is thick, thin with water to the consistency of cream. Use no more than two colors of paint at one time. If more colors are desired, let the lampshade dry, clean the pan, and repeat the steps.

2 **Use a skewer** to gently swirl the paints in the starch. Do not overmix. The paint will float on top of the starch.

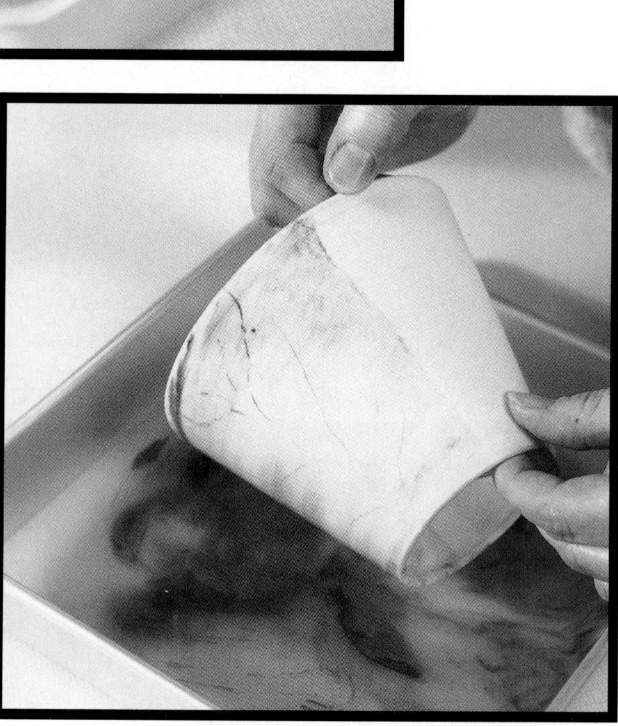

3 **Carefully roll the lampshade** over the surface of the liquid. For darker designs, hold the shade in the solution longer.

4 **Remove lampshade** from the pan and let dry on waxed paper.

1 more idea...

- For an even more artistic rendition, add hand-painted touches over the marbleizing.

also try this...

- Top a sports-theme lamp with a shade painted in team colors.

good ideas *butterfly candles*

Dress up everyday pillar candles with artificial butterflies. Available on wires, these butterflies poke right into the surface of the candle to add a summery, outdoor touch. Be sure to keep these fluttering beauties away from the direct flame of the candle.

bubble wands

To make a bubble wand you will need:
- Star-shape cookie cutter
- 40-inch piece of 20-gauge wire
- Wire cutters
- Electric drill
- Spray paint in desired color

Send airy bubbles afloat on summer breezes with these star-spangled bubble wands.

here's how **To make this project,** fold a 40-inch piece of wire in half. Starting at one point of the star, bend the wire around the cookie cutter to form the star outline. When the wire meets, twist to secure.

Straighten the ends of the wire and trim them with wire cutters to make them an even length. Insert the trimmed ends into the chuck on an electric drill and tighten the chuck. Hold the wire taut and rotate the drill until the wire is twisted to the desired tightness. Loosen the chuck and remove the wire. Trim the ends again.

Carefully remove the star from the cookie cutter. Spray-paint the star. Let the paint dry.

1 more idea...
- Decorate your deck for the Fourth of July with the wands.

also try this...
- Transform the bubble wands into napkin holders by wrapping the handle around an empty paper towel tube to make a ring.

charming note cards

Trimmed with decorative-edge scissors, these summer-hue papers create a soft background for gold metal charms.

To make a note card you will need:
Medium-weight papers in yellow, pale green, medium green, periwinkle blue, and purple for the summer cards shown here; *or* cream, taupe, gold, purple, lavender, and pale lavender as shown on the front cover
Straight-edge and decorative-edge scissors
Thick white crafts glue
Gold metal charms with desired motifs
Needle-nose pliers

here's how **To make this project,** use straight-edge scissors to cut a 9¼×5⅛-inch piece of yellow paper for the square card or a 6⅝×5½-inch piece of pale green paper for the rectangular card. Fold the paper in half with the short ends aligned. Crease the fold. (See the *front cover* for alternate color choices.)

For the square card, use decorative-edge scissors to cut a medium green piece of paper 8×4 inches. Fold in half with the short ends aligning. Glue over the yellow piece of paper. Cut four 1¼-inch squares, 2 from yellow and 2 from pale green. Center and glue on front of card, leaving ⅛ inch between squares.

For the rectangular card, use straight scissors to cut a 4½×2½-inch piece of blue paper. Glue atop purple paper, leaving ¼ inch on each side. Trim the purple paper close to blue paper using decorative-edge scissors. Glue in center of card front. Cut a ⅞×3⅛-inch piece from pale green. Glue in center of card front.

Remove hanging loops from charms if necessary by bending with a pliers. Glue charms on card front as desired. Let the glue dry.

1 more idea...

- Sew the charms on the card using coordinating thread.

also try this...

- Spruce up homemade note cards with colorful buttons.

bulb bowls

To make flower bulbs blooming gorgeous, nest them in a painted dish filled with interesting marbles.

To make a bulb bowl you will need:

Star-shape or other terra-cotta dish at least 1½ inches deep
Yellow acrylic paint
Paintbrush
Colored aquarium gravel
Colored marbles
Paper white narcissus bulbs

here's how **To make this project,** paint the dish with yellow acrylic paint. Let it dry. Apply a second and third coat if needed. Let the paint dry.

Fill the dish with colored aquarium gravel. Outline the edges with colored marbles.

Press several bulbs into the gravel until the roots are below the gravel and the bulbs sit stably. The bulbs do not have to be completely buried.

When ready to start the bulbs, fill the dish with water, always keeping the roots well soaked. The flowers will bloom in about 2 weeks.

1 more idea...

- To give as a gift, wrap the dish in clear or transparent-color cellophane, gathering the cellophane in the center and tying with a ribbon.

also try this...

- Instead of using flower bulbs, place a large pillar candle in the center of the dish.

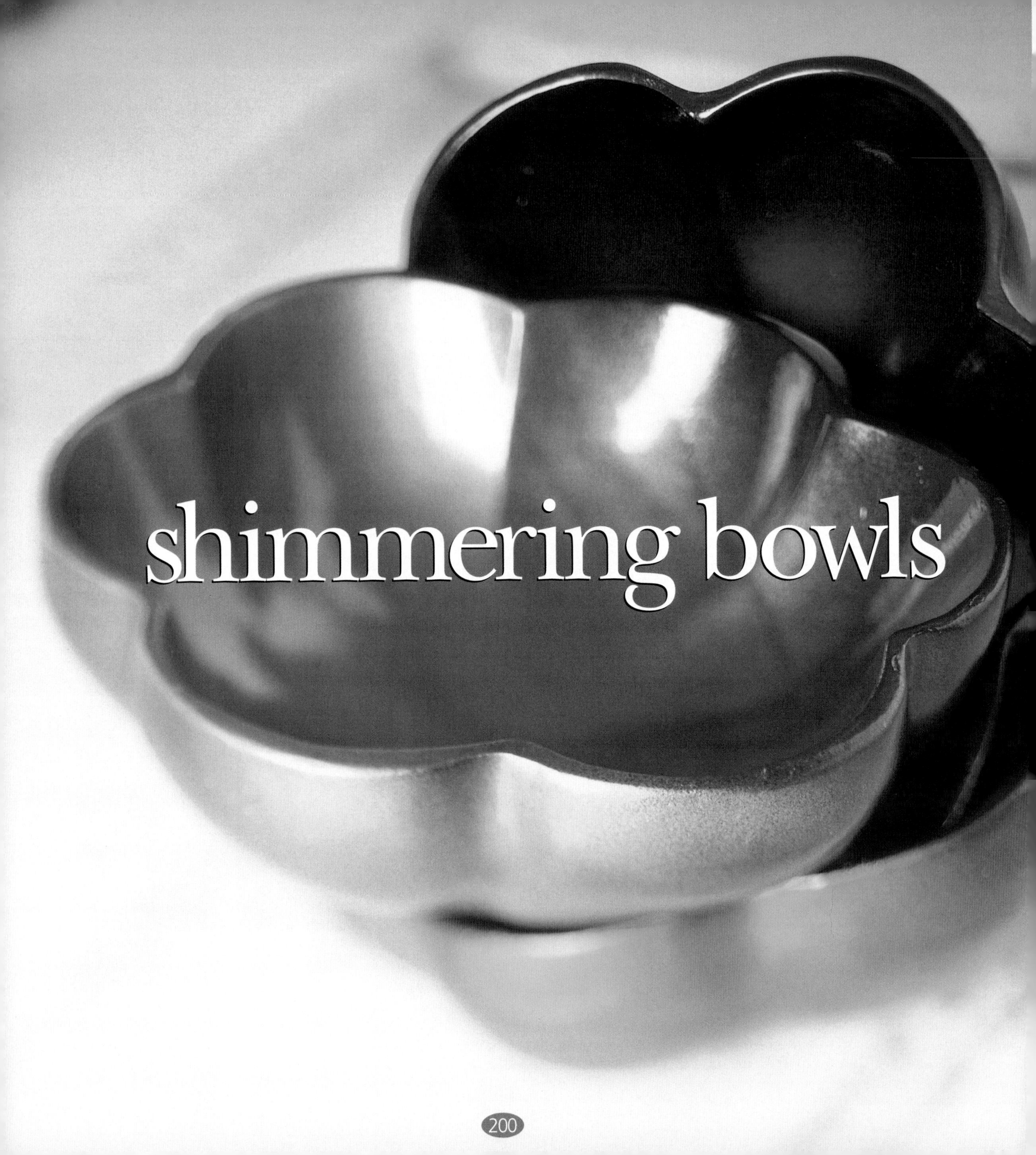

shimmering bowls

Layers of transparent paints give a fresh glow to garage-sale wood bowls.

To make a bowl you will need:
Wood bowl
White spray primer
Bright gold spray paint
Transparent spray paints in yellow, green, blue, and red

1 **Wash and dry the bowl.** Spray the bowl with a light coat of white spray primer. Let it dry.

2 **Spray the bowl** with a light coat of bright gold spray paint. Let it dry. Turn over the bowl and spray the other side. Let it dry. Apply a second coat and let it dry.

3 **Spray half of the bowl one color,** such as green, beginning at the far end and fading off toward the center. Spray more heavily on the far end. The transparent paint allows the gold to show through, achieving a more metallic color. Let it dry.

4 **Spray the remaining half** a contrasting color, such as blue. Begin at the opposite end, spraying evenly and lightly until the colors overlap, creating a third color. Let the paint dry.

5 **Turn over the bowl** and paint the outside in the same manner as used on the inside of the bowl. Let the paint dry.

NOTE: Do not use bowls for unwrapped foods.

1 more idea...

- Use these transparent paints on other wood projects, such as picture frames and stools.

also try this...

- To add a handle to the bowl, drill holes in opposite sides of the bowl and use heavy wire or lead-free solder to shape a handle.

make it in minutes

cherry jar topper

Homemade jams and jellies make much-appreciated gifts, especially when wrapped with this lovely jar topper.

To make a jar topper you will need:
- Circle of fabric, approximately 4 inches wider in diameter than jar top
- Scissors
- Thick white crafts glue
- Decorative rickrack
- Circle of rubber shelf lining, 1 inch smaller in diameter than jar top
- Pencil
- Lightweight cardboard
- Drill and 1/16-inch drill bit
- Two 1-inch-diameter wood balls
- Red acrylic paint
- Paintbrush
- 6-inch-long piece of green plastic-coated wire
- Green felt
- 20 inches of 1/4-inch-wide ribbon

here's how **To make this project,** cut a circle from fabric that is 4 inches wider in diameter than jar top. Glue rickrack around the edge, trimming rickrack to fit. Glue the rubber liner circle in the center of the fabric. Let the glue dry.

Trace the top of the jar lid onto the cardboard. Cut out the circle. Glue the cardboard piece in the center of the fabric circle on the wrong side. Let the glue dry.

To make the cherries, drill a 1/2-inch-deep hole in each wood ball. Paint the wood balls red. Let the paint dry. Apply a second coat if necessary. Let dry.

Fold the wire piece in half. Glue the ends of the wire in the holes in the wood balls. Let the glue dry.

Cut a 6×2-inch piece from green felt. Fold with short ends together. Cut a leaf shape, leaving 1/2 inch at fold. This will create two connected leaves. Tie the green felt shape in the center of the wire. Glue the cherries in the center of the rubber circle. Let the glue dry.

Place the topper over the jar. Place ribbon around jar top, approximately 1/2 inch from the top. Tie into a bow.

1 more idea...
- For a quicker version of this project, purchase artificial cherries, apples, pears, or other miniature fruits to glue to the jar topper.

also try this...
- Add a pretty spoon to this gift by tying it to the ribbon bow.

star-rimmed basket

Perfect for toting Fourth of July picnic goodies, this whitewashed basket is trimmed with precut wood stars painted in patriotic red and blue.

To make a basket you will need:

Basket
White stain gel
Paintbrush
Disposable foam plates
Acrylic paints in barn red and navy
Wood stars 1 to $2\frac{1}{2}$ inches wide
Fine sandpaper
Tack cloth
Hot-glue gun and hot-glue stick

here's how **To make this project,** paint the basket using white stain gel and a wide flat brush. Place some gel on a foam plate. Paint vertical strokes until well covered. Let the stain gel dry. Paint another coat if a more opaque color is desired.

Put a dab of barn red and navy blue paint on plate. Thin the paint with water, about one part paint to one part water. Paint the stars. Let the paint dry.

Using fine sandpaper, lightly sand the stars. Sand the edges to create a worn look. Brush off dust and wipe with a tack cloth.

Using hot glue, layer contrasting small stars over large stars.

Hot-glue stars onto rim of basket, alternating colors and sizes of stars.

1 more idea...

- For a picnic, place silverware in patriotic paper napkins, tie with ribbon, and use the basket as a holder.

also try this...

- To change the rim design for different seasons, attach the stars with circles of hook-and-loop tape, such as Velcro.

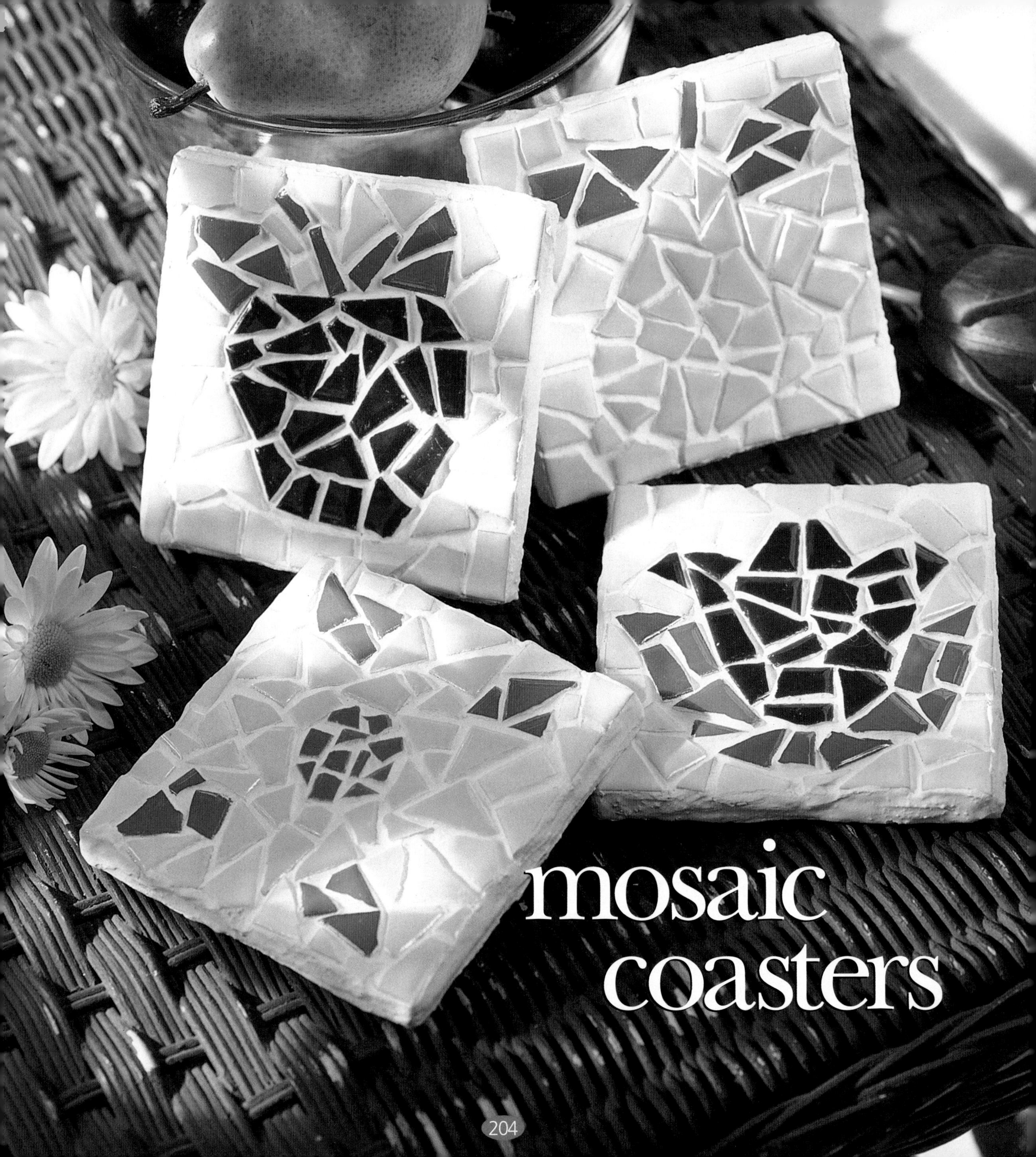

mosaic coasters

With designs inspired by Mother Nature, these fun-to-make coasters will help you master the technique of tiling.

To make the coasters you will need:
Tracing paper
Pencil
Carbon paper
Four 4⅜-inch-square ceramic tiles
Permanent marking pen
Safety glasses
Tile-cutting nipper
Hammer
Towel
Tiles, such as Plaid Mosaics Bags o' Chips (1 bag each of red, orange, green, and yellow, and 2 bags of white)
Crafts stick
Tile adhesive
White sanded tile grout
Spatula
Sponge

1 **Trace the patterns,** *pages 206–207,* onto tracing paper. Use carbon paper to transfer the designs to the center of each tile. Trace over the carbon paper lines using marking pen.

2 **Protect eyes with safety glasses.** To break the tiles, use a cutting nipper or hammer. To break tile with a hammer, put tiles on a towel with the colored surface down. Tap with a hammer.

3 **Using the patterns** as color guides, glue the appropriate tiles inside the marking pen lines. Use a crafts stick to spread tile adhesive on the back of the tile pieces as you go. Fill in around the patterns using white tile pieces.

4 **Mix grout according** to the manufacturer's instructions. Spread grout on top of the tiles with a spatula and fingers, pressing grout in the spaces between tiles.

5 **Wipe grout off** the top of the tiles with a damp sponge. Let the grout set. Mix additional grout and spread around the edges of the coaster. Smooth the edges with your fingers.

1 more idea...
- Look in coloring books for more patterns to use when doing mosaic tiling.

also try this...
- Make trivets in the same manner, using a larger tile for the base.

mosaic coasters (continued)

pretty floral bag

These sturdy, floral totes are as lovely as they are practical.

To make a bag you will need:

- Scissors
- ¾ yard of the main fabric
- ¼ yard of contrast fabric
- 1 yard lining fabric
- Thread to coordinate with fabric
- 3×3-inch doily or appliqué
- 2 buttons for trim

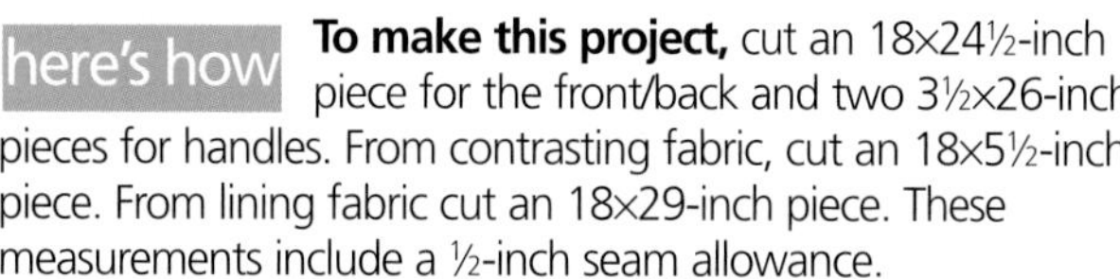

here's how **To make this project,** cut an 18×24½-inch piece for the front/back and two 3½×26-inch pieces for handles. From contrasting fabric, cut an 18×5½-inch piece. From lining fabric cut an 18×29-inch piece. These measurements include a ½-inch seam allowance.

Stitch the contrasting fabric to the front/back piece along one 18-inch side. Fold the front/back with contrasting fabric in half crosswise. Mark the bottom fold on each side. Mark 3 inches up from the fold at the sides. With right sides facing, refold the bottom of the bag on the 3-inch marks so the bottom fold of the bag is 3 inches above the new folds.

For handles, press in ½ inch along each long side of handle fabric. Fold in half lengthwise and topstitch. Baste the handles to the front and back, 5 inches in from side seams.

Stitch the lining in the same manner as the bag, eliminating the contrasting fabric and handles, and leaving an opening in one side seam for turning.

With right sides facing, match side seams and keep handles free. Stitch lining to bag around the top edge. Turn the bag through the lining opening. Press the lining to the inside of the bag. Stitch the lining opening closed.

Center and stitch or fuse doily or appliqué to the contrasting fabric. If fusing, apply according to the manufacturer's instructions. Add decorative buttons atop doily or appliqué.

1 more idea...

- Use playful prints to make travel totes for children.

also try this...

- Recycle denim jeans to make sturdy bags to carry portable crafts projects.

more ideas *for* summer

- Align your walkway with small colorful metal sand pails. Fill halfway with sand and add a votive candle to make summer luminarias.
- Spend the day at a riverbank and take along your sketch pad.
- Pick fresh blooms and press in a heavy book until dry. Use these prepared flowers to make note cards.
- Visit an outdoor flea market, keeping an eye out for unusual containers to use as vases.
- Spray-paint watering cans to use as colorful vases for the porch and patio.
- At the end of the season, purchase a sale-priced picnic basket to keep crafts supplies in while traveling.

- Visit your local bookstore to explore new crafts magazines and books.
- Choose an easy project in this chapter and teach a group of children how to make it.
- Align vintage milk bottles on a windowsill, placing a single flower in each.
- Before tossing any outgrown clothing, use good sections to make a memory quilt.
- Watch fabric-store sales for good buys on printed pastel ribbons to weave for a pillow top.
- Create a wreath using dried flowers from the garden.

glossary

Acrylic paint—available in hundreds of colors, this water-based paint is commonly used to paint wood and paper items.

Aida—available in white or colors and in a variety of squares per inch, this cross-stitch fabric is woven to create tiny squares to make stitching easy.

Bakeable clay—available in white or a variety of colors in art, crafts, and discount stores, this type of clay hardens only when baked in the oven.

Band saw—a power saw in the form of an endless steel belt running over pulleys.

Batting—layers or sheets of raw cotton, wool, or polyester used for lining quilts or for stuffing items, such as pillows or dolls.

Beaded garland—sold on a spool or by the yard, this is a garland in which the beads are stationary and joined by string or thread.

Beading wire—a fine wire that is thin enough to thread through the holes in most beads.

Bobby pins—a crimped, folded piece of wire to hold hair in place.

Bugle beads—a small cylinder bead made of glass or plastic that comes in a variety of lengths and colors.

Card stock—heavy paper that is used for making cards and other craft projects.

Chenille stems—similar to pipe cleaners, these bendable stems come in a variety of colors, sizes, and designs.

Clear acrylic spray—a clear spray used as a coating to protect surfaces.

Cording—a slender, flexible material usually consisting of several strands of thread woven or twisted together.

Crackling medium—a paint-on liquid that is applied between two coats of different paint colors to create a crackling effect.

Crafting foam—sheets of foam that range in thicknesses and color.

Crafts knife—a small hand tool with a sharp replaceable blade to cut intricate designs.

Decorative-edge scissors—scissors that have shaped blades that create a pattern when used, such as scallops and zigzags.

Decoupage—the art of decorating surfaces by applying cutouts (as of paper) and then coating with several layers of finish.

Dowel—a round rod or stick used for woodworking.

Embroidery floss—used for cross-stitch, embroidery, and other crafting projects, this skein of thread is composed of six plies of thread.

Etching cream—an acid cream used to frost glass.

Fabric paint or paint pen—available in tubes at crafts, discount, and fabric stores, this paint can be applied directly from the tube or put on a disposable plate and painted onto the surface.

Fiberfill—synthetic fibers used as a filling material for items such as pillows, cushions, and padded picture frames.

Finial—an ornamental topper, such as those used at the tops of lamps and newel posts.

Flat marbles—often used for floral arranging, these glass marbles are flat and can be purchased translucent or opaque.

Floral spray paint— a spray paint that is made exclusively to change the color of fresh flowers.

Fusible webbing—a strong, closely woven material that can be bonded to something when heated with an iron.

Gesso—Found with painting supplies, this paint-on liquid is usually used to prepare surfaces to accept paint.

Glass cement—strong clear adhesive formulated to work on glass.

Glass paint—formulated for use on glass, these water-based paints can be applied with a brush and may need to be baked in the oven to become permanent.

Glitter—available in a variety of colors, this embellishment is usually glued onto a surface where color, texture, and sparkle are wanted.

Glue stick—a soft, solid glue that is often used to bond papers.

Grout—a thin mortar used for filling spaces when doing tiling projects.

Hot-glue gun—a handheld crafting tool that melts glue sticks and has a trigger-controlled grip to release melted glue from the tip of the gun. There are also low-temp guns and glues available that work in the same manner.

Hot-glue stick—solid sticks of glue that melt when inserted into a hot-glue gun.

Instant-bond glue—a clear, strong adhesive that bonds upon contact.

Model car paint—available in a bottle or as a spray paint, these paints come in a variety of colors.

Motif—a dominant idea or central theme; a single or repeated design or color.

Needle-nose pliers—a small pincer for holding small objects or bending and cutting wire.

Paper crimper—a handheld crafting tool that creates ridges in paper, resembling corrugated cardboard.

Paper tube—an emptied holder for paper toweling.

Plastic foam or Styrofoam—usually white or green, these porous foam pieces come in a variety of shapes and sizes for crafting purposes.

Quilting pins—available at crafts, discount, and fabric stores, these straight pins are long with a large, round plastic head.

Rhinestones—faceted glass or plastic jewellike trims used for decoration on crafts or clothing.

Rubber cement—a glue that can be used for temporary adhesion or coverage and then rubbed off.

Rubber stamps—available in hundreds of designs, these stamps can be used with ink or paint to transfer designs to desired surfaces.

Running stitch—a small even stitch running in and out of cloth.

Screw eye—a pointed screw with the head shaped into a circle.

Scrollsaw—a power handsaw with a thin blade used for cutting curves or irregular designs.

Seed beads—tiny round beads that usually require a beading needle for attaching to an item.

Self-adhesive vinyl—often used to cover shelves, this vinyl has a paper backing which is removed to reveal a sticky surface on the back of the vinyl.

Sequins—available in a variety of shapes and sizes, these small glittering trims have a hole in the middle so they can be sewn in place.

Solder—usually sold in spools for soldering, this lead-free cord can be shaped and used for ornamentation on crafts.

Sponge brushes—available with a plastic or wood handle, these disposable paintbrushes have a solid foam piece in place of bristles.

Tack cloth—a sticky cloth usually used to remove sawdust from a surface.

Terra-cotta flower pot—a dull orange-color clay pot.

Thick white crafts glue—a sticky white glue that dries clear and can be used on fabric, paper, wood, plastic foam, and most plastic surfaces.

Tracing paper—a thin, transparent paper that can be easily seen through to trace a line pattern when placed underneath.

Votive candle—a small, squat candle.

Waterproof sealer—available in a spray or to paint on, this sealer will protect an object from water.

Whipstitch—a shallow overcasting stitch often used to join two fabric pieces.

Wire cutters—a hand tool used to cut through wires.

Wire-edged ribbon—available in many widths and colors in fabric, crafts, and discount stores, this ribbon is edged with fine wire so it will maintain a desired shape.

Wood skewer—a long, wood rod with a pointed end to poke through foods or other surfaces.

index

sources

Photographers:
Peter Krumhardt, Scott Little, Andy Lyons Cameraworks

Photo Styling: Carol Dahlstrom
Photo Styling Assistant: Donna Chesnut

Designers:
Susan Banker: Pages 12–14, 20, 25, 30, 32–33, 35, 40, 50, 62, 66, 83, 87–88, 102–103, 107–111, 114–115, 126, 138, 145, 153, 171, 188–191, 198, 202.

Donna Chesnut: Pages 26–27, 150–151, 186–187, 197.

Carol Dahlstrom: Pages 16–17, 65, 70–71, 72, 78, 84–85, 94–95, 162–163, 177, 178, 182–183, 197.

Phyllis Dobbs: Pages 21, 204.

Phyllis Dunstan: Pages 53, 64, 68, 74, 79, 91, 105, 127, 135, 149, 152, 178, 192, 194–195.

Alice Okon: Page 80.

Margaret Sindelar: Pages 116–117, 166–168, 208.

Alice Wetzel: Pages 10, 14–15,18, 31, 34, 36–37, 42, 45–48, 56, 82, 96–101, 113, 118–121, 128–133, 136, 140–142, 148, 154–158, 164, 170, 181, 184, 199, 200, 203.

If you liked this book...

look for...

Simply Handmade:
365 Easy Gifts & Decorations You Can Make
wherever quality books are sold.